The Magic of
Beaded Spherical Nets:

Techniques and Projects

By

Merry Makela

Honey Beads Press, College Station

Published by
Archer Ellison Publishing
P.O. Box 9167
College Station, TX 77842
(409) 693-0331
(409) 694-6715 - fax

In cooperation with
Honey Beads Press
P. O. Box 13464
College Station, TX 77841-6464

Front and Back Cover Photography by
Tracy Amthor Abeel, Halfmoon Photography

Manufactured in the United States of America

Makela, Merry
Beaded Nets

ISBN 1-57472-201-8

To
Pat Patterson
for all the good humored support he has given
and to
Pitiful Awful Cat
for his unfailing appreciation
of himself.

Acknowledgements

I would like to thank several people for their help and encouragement in the preparation of this book for publication. Alice Scherer, director of the Center for the Study of Beadwork, which publishes "Notes from a BEADWORKERS JOURNAL", gets a healthy hug for all of her helpful suggestions and meticulous editing of the first, but eventually discarded, draft. She then went on to recruit several of her friends as beta testers for the instructional chapters of my second attempt. My heartfelt thanks go out to these testers: Cheryl Aufderheide, Frieda Bates (and her dislike for wobbly ear studs), Ezgi Bozkurt, Mary Cave, Barbara Grainger (Appendix B is for you, friend), Teddy Rainwater, and Frances Ross. Finally, I would like to thank Allen and Kim D'Angelo of Archer-Ellison Publishing who took me by the hand and brought this project to a successful conclusion.

Preface

Seed beads have always been my passion. My first ones were opaques in various colors that came in little glass tubes with real cork stoppers. The passion lay dormant from childhood until ten years ago when I started a bead business from my home during a lull in my real (?) career. The idea that eventually led to spherical nets, started as a desire to make seed bead covers for larger beads. I wanted a method that was quick and easy so I wouldn't need to spend a lot of time wondering what the next bead should be. The results were the first ball nets. As time passed I made more nets, squashing them and mangling them in various ways until the flat nets began to take on their final shapes. I knew by then that the spherical net method was generalizable and adaptable to many uses. Finally, I took the plunge and started making the really big spherical nets into baskets and bottle covers.

Even before the basket/bottle cover phase, I knew I had to write a book. Writing is not my favorite activity (I need an "I'd rather be beading" sticker for my computer), but I wanted to share the method of spherical nets with other beaders. Mainly because no one ever believed me that a 2 inch diameter, beaded double sided disk took about an hour to construct and was easy.

So I wrote the book. I've included most of what I know about the basics of spherical nets. Chapter 1 has a list of the tools and supplies you will need. Chapter 2 shows you how to make your first sherical net which is a beaded cover for a 12 mm bead. This chapter also contains a detailed discussion of the various parts of a spherical net and some extraneous rules that you won't be tested on.

In Chapter 3 you will make a flat net which is constructed in much the same manner as a ball net but instead of inserting an interior bead prior to closing, a flat net is closed first and then "flattened" and "anchored". The result is a two-layered disk with the spokes radiating out from the center of the circle. You will learn how to anchor this structure into a disk that is so stiff you will have a hard time convincing your friends it is not made with wire.

In Chapter 4 you will learn two methods of making stud earrings out of flat nets. Chapter 5 will teach you how fringes can be attached to flat nets to make earrings and pins. Chapter 6 contains instructions for making a two-layered, stand-alone basket and a simple cover for a bottle. This will complete the basics of spherical nets and related techniques.

The last three chapters of the book contain variations on the basics. In Chapter 7 you will learn how to make several projects out of ball nets of different sizes including a pair of earrings out of drop nets. In Chapter 8 you will find several sizes of flat nets for earrings and pins. Chapter 9 has some additional patterns for baskets, covered bottles and a Christmas tree ornament.

I have had a great deal of fun in the past six years playing with these beaded shapes and discovering new and sometimes useful variations. The failures are often more instructive than the successes. At any rate I have kept all of them in my pattern box. My husband has dutifully admired many incomprehensible wads of beads as I have expounded on the latest interesting variation. My hope is that you will also find pleasure and interest in constructing spherical nets and that you will eventually shelve this volume for good as you expand your repertoire of variations beyond those I have described.

Contents

1 Introduction to Spherical Nets

The purpose of this book is to introduce you to the concept of beaded spherical nets and teach you how variations on the basic concept can be made into an amazing array of jewelry items and small objects d'art. The term "spherical net" is a general term for this family of shapes composed mostly of seed beads and thread. The "spherical" part of the name comes from the fact that as the net is being constructed, it curls naturally into a spherical shape. The <u>final</u> shape, however, may be round, teardrop, flat or complexly curved, depending on the primary sequence of beads and the final anchoring treatment.

These are the final shapes that will be taught in this book. The cover shows 6 out of 21 spherical nets for which there are explicit patterns.

Ball nets are the simplest spherical nets since they require no finishing steps except tying off the two ends of the thread. In general they are round and require an interior bead to "fill them out" and keep the spherical shape. The first spherical net you will make is a ball net that covers a 12 mm interior bead. Patterns are included in Chapter 7 for ball nets that cover 16 and 20 mm interior beads.

Teardrop nets or just plain drop nets are very similar to ball nets in construction technique in that they require no finishing steps except tying off. They also require an interior bead to hold their shape. Since teardrop shaped beads are more difficult to find than round ones, a technique for substituting a stack of round beads on a head pin will be presented. A pattern for a teardrop net that uses a 12 mm round bead as part of its interior columnar framework is detailed in Chapter 7.

Flat nets are the most versatile of finished shapes. They do not take an interior bead since the space that the interior bead would occupy is lost in the flattening step. A center bead, however, usually sits in the center of the flat net, either as an added decoration or to hold or hide the earring stud. Flat nets are double sided disks that are very stiff and hold their shape without interior shapers used in ball and teardrop nets. The size of a flat net depends on how many beads are used in each part of the net. Patterns are included for flat nets that range from 7/8 inch in

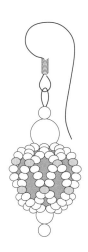

—— Types of —— Spherical Nets

Ball Nets

Teardrop Nets

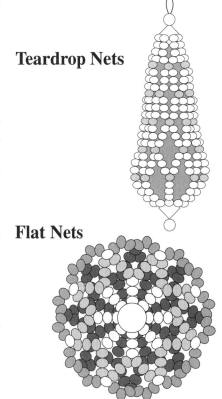

Flat Nets

diameter to 2.0 inches. Because they are made almost entirely of seed beads, they are relatively lightweight so even the largest flat net can be made into earrings. A flat net can be used alone as a disk or serve as a base for a fringe. Fringes will be introduced in Chapter 5.

Baskets

Baskets are the largest spherical nets and consist of an outer layer and an inner lining. They are not used as items of personal adornment since I have not yet figured out how. They are impressive, however, in that they hold their shape without an interior bead or other item. Two patterns for baskets are included: one with a flaring rim like a vase which is detailed in Chapter 9 and the second, rimless like an Indian pot, in Chapters 6 and 9.

Bottle Covers

Bottle covers are similar to ball nets except that they are much larger. They are perhaps the easiest of all bottle covers to make since the precise fitting of beads to bottle is a lot easier (see Chapter 6, a word on net stretchability). The technique is discussed in detail for a bottle cover for a 3/4 oz. plastic "white-out" bottle in Chapter 6. Two more esthetically pleasing bottle covers are given in Chapter 9, along with a pattern for covering a glass Christmas tree ornament.

—— Supplies ——

Most of the projects described in the following chapters require a minimum of supplies. Sources for all supplies and items in the next section can be found in Appendix A: Sources for Supplies.

Needles

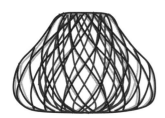

For all spherical nets, John James brand #12 sharps (1.125 inches long) are recommended. These are thin enough to go through most seed beads and yet have large enough eyes to accommodate upholstery nylon thread. These needles are used for the bodies of the spherical nets because they are stiff enough to get between very tightly packed beads for the final tying off. On the other hand, size 13 "Best Quality Beading Needles" from England which are thinner and longer (2.0 inches) are recommended for fringes (see Chapter 5).

Thread

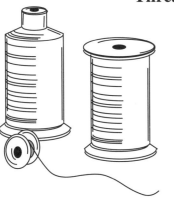

The best thread for spherical nets is nylon "Bead Thread" size "C" or Nymo size "D" made by Belding. These threads are easy to thread into the #12 needles, but come in a limited set of colors and may be difficult to find. Upholstery nylon, on the other hand, is about a size "E" and, therefore, more difficult to thread into the John James #12 needles. However, it comes in a variety of colors and is readily available in most fabric shops. I prefer thread made by "Conso" as it is stiffer and easier to get through the needle's eye. **Do not use Kevlar**. It is thin and strong, but tends to cut itself if two threads cross at right angles.

Seed Beads

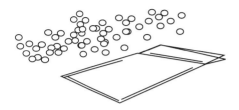

Seed beads sizes 9/0, 10/0 and 11/0 have large enough holes, especially those made in Japan, to accommodate the needles and threads discussed above. In addition they are the correct size to make a final product of the size discussed in the following chapters. Larger and smaller seed beads may be used, but the size of final product will vary accordingly.

Unlike many seed bead patterns, spherical nets do not require beads of different colors to be all the same size. Regular and 3-cut Czech seed beads of sizes 10/0 and 11/0 can be mixed with Japanese 11/0 beads in a single piece. The result is an interesting mixture of colors and textures. The patterns in the early chapters use specific colors of seed beads as instructional aids. Later patterns use more interesting color combinations.

Center Beads

4 5 6 7 8 10 12

In many of the flat net patterns (Chapters 3, 4, 5 and 8) a center bead is used either to hide or carry the wire that serves as the earring or tie-tack stud. Depending on the size of the flat net, center beads range from 4 mm to 8 mm in diameter. Round or round-faceted glass or stone beads are preferred. Round-faceted crystals are very pretty.

Interior Beads

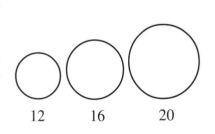

12 16 20

In patterns that are not flattened, an interior bead is often used to hold the shape of the spherical net. Interior beads can be round or teardrop shaped. In some patterns, a column of beads on a head pin will serve. Interior beads are not actually attached to the spherical net, but are put inside the net just before the final closing. Interior beads used in this book range from 12 to 20 mm although any size can be accommodated.

Earring Studs

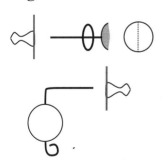

Most patterns of flat nets call for stud earrings. These are of two types: off-center and central. Off-center studs can be made from 20 gauge wire. See Appendix A: Sources of Supplies for sources of 20 gauge, half-hard, gold-filled or silver wire. Central studs are either 4 mm cupped or 6 mm flat studs, usually of surgical steel, which can be purchased commercially. 6 mm flat studs don't wobble as much as the 4 mm cups do. Central studs also require 4 mm soldered jump rings. The use of the soldered rings and how to make them are discussed in Chapter 4. All studs earrings use comfort clutches.

Earring Clips

Some earrings that are made as studs can instead be made with ear clips for non-pierced ears. Ear clips with 15 mm perforated bases can be sewn to the backs of flat nets (instructions in Chapter 8). Earrings made of ball or teardrop nets can be hung from earring findings for non-pierced ears.

Pinning Mechanisms

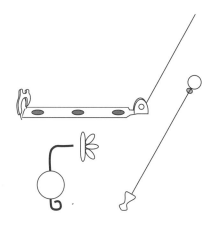

Most of the larger flat nets can be made into pins. One inch commercial pin backs with perforated bases can be sewn to the backs of flat nets. Sometimes, however, the pin backs show through the spaces in the flat net and detract from the beauty of the pin. An alternative method is to use a stick pin to secure the flat net to the garment. Stick pins can be made from stiff 3 inch head pins or from 20 gauge, half-hard, gold-filled or silver wire. One end of the stick pin has a 5 or 6 mm bead held in place with either glue or a crimp bead. The other end is sharpened and then protected by an ear clutch, preferrably the type known as a "comfort clutch", but without the plastic collar. A pattern for a 2 inch flat net that uses a stick pin is given in Chapter 8. A third pin mechanism is similar to off-center ear studs. The wire, however, is 18 gauge, sharpened and held in place with a tie-tack back. The fringed pin in Chapter 5 and the large plain pin in Chapter 8 use this mechanism.

Bottles, Vases & Ornaments

Be on the lookout for interesting and unusual bottles, small vases and plain Christmas tree ornaments. Two good sources of bottles and vases are listed in Appendix A: Sources of Supplies. Christmas tree ornaments are available in craft stores just before Christmas. These items should have a round cross section. That is, if you sliced the bottle parallel to the ground, the cut surface would be a circle. Also it must have a "shoulder". This means that the net must have something to close in on near the top of the bottle so the whole net won't slip off. For this reason, U-shaped vases are not suitable. The two bottle covers in Chapter 9 illustrate the range of variation that bottle covers can take. The 6 inch bottle has a low shoulder and very long neck while the 4.5 inch bottle is nearly cylindrical with a high shoulder. The Christmas tree ornament is bell shaped.

——Tools & Other —— Stuff

The following tools and supplies that are useful in making spherical nets:

Bead Gauge

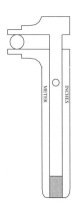

A bead gauge is a very handy gadget that can be used to measure the diameter of beads. The one pictured is made of brass and has inch as well as centimeter and millimeter markings. There are 1000 millimeters in a meter and 100 centimeters. Therefore, one centimeter = 10 millimeters. Millimeter units are abbreviated mm (and centimeter, cm) so that a 6 mm bead is 6 millimeters or 0.6 centimeters in diameter. Most glass and stone beads are measured in mm. Some of the larger dimensions in this book are given in inches. An approximate conversion of inches to mm is 1 inch = 25 mm = 2.5 cm.

Sandpaper

A four inch square piece of black carbide sandpaper (200 - 400 grit) is handy for many things, including smoothing the ends of wires used as off-center ear studs and sharpening the ends of wires used as pins.

Glues

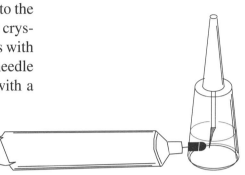

Some beaders use clear glue in tying off to secure knots in their threads and when the glue is dry, they clip the thread close to the knot. A number of clear glues can be used, including watch crystal glue and clear nail polish. The watch crystal glue comes with a very fine point applicator that is kept clear with a fine needle attached to the cap. Clear nail polish should be applied with a needle or other pointed object since the brush it comes with is so wide you get polish in inappropriate places. Alternatively, you can trim the nail polish brush at an angle with a pair of scissors so it comes to a fine point. You can also thin the polish with nail polish remover.

Matches

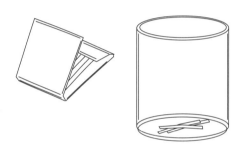

Instead of using glue, some beaders (including myself) prefer to clip the thread about 1/4 inches from the knot and burn the thread down to the knot. This will only work with <u>nylon</u> threads, however. Most upholstery threads and Nymo are nylon and can be burned down. If you use this method, be sure to wear eye protection, use paper rather than wooden matches and always discard the used match in a special container, not a waste-paper basket. I keep a special jar by my work table just for used matches. Paper matches are better than wooden because they burn longer and with a smaller flame than wooden matches, so the process is more controllable.

Soldering Irons

A soldering iron is used to make soldered rings which are incorporated into flat nets for central stud earrings. A small iron with a wire stand is recommended and can be purchased in almost any hardware store. The best solder is Staybright by J.W. Harris Co. available in jeweler's supply stores. Instructions for making and using soldered rings are given in Chapter 4.

Pliers and Tweezers

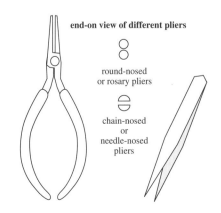

end-on view of different pliers

round-nosed
or rosary pliers

chain-nosed
or
needle-nosed
pliers

Pliers and tweezers are essential beading tools. In making spherical nets, pliers are handy for pulling a needle through snug fitting beads. Round-nosed, or rosary pliers, are used to make loops in wires for off-center stud earrings and tie-tack pins. Chain, long or needle-nose pliers come in two styles: smooth and serrated. Pliers with a smooth gripping surface will not scar the wire as it is being manipulated. Pliers with small serrations on the gripping surface are necessary for tasks where smooth pliers slip such as in closing wire loops and jump-rings. A pair of wire cutters is also handy.

Crimping Tool

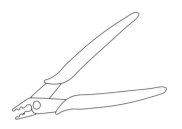

A new type of pliers came on the market a few years ago. These are known as crimping tools. A crimping tool can be used on one project: the flat net pin that is held in place with a three inch hat-pin type pin. See Chapter 8 for details. When buying a crimping tool, look for a pair where the two jaws come together exactly on line. If the two jaws tend to miss one-another even a little, they won't close your crimp beads squarely. This is more than a little annoying.

Pattern Boxes

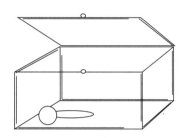

As a pattern developer, I have made many pieces that have not made their way into this book. But I still have each and every one of them in my pattern box. Many times I have fished an old piece out of the box to study how I approached a particular problem in the past. Some of these old pieces have been developed into new ideas. The point is that since seed beads are relatively inexpensive, it is a better idea to save your practice and "failed" pieces which can serve as bases for later study.

Glasses, Lamps, Work Desks, Chairs, and Other Opinions

I am farsighted and need glasses to see my beadwork. I have a special pair of very strong glasses that I use only to do beadwork. They stay at my bead desk mainly because I get sea-sick trying to negotiate the stairs with them on.

The desk where I work has two swing-arm lamps: one which takes a regular bulb and the other, a circular fluorescent bulb which surrounds a magnifying glass. The magnifying glass comes in very handy when threading needles and finishing pieces.

My desk is a 3x5 foot piece of 3/4 inch plywood, covered with an old bed pad and "Naugahyde". For you youngens, Naugahyde is what passed for fake leather a few (ha!) years ago. It serves as a giant pin cushion. An added benefit is that beads don't bounce much on this surface. I use an 18 inch ruler to serve as a levee to keep beads from rolling off the desk. This is handy since I don't use bead trays, but pour my beads out directly onto the desk surface. In my opinion, bead trays make it difficult keep beads on your needle while you pick up others. A flat surface, with maybe a little texture to keep beads from rolling, is best for fast, efficient beadwork.

My chair is ergonomically designed for people who sit for long periods of time. It cost a bundle. But it is worth every penny and my back thanks me every night.

2 Ball Nets and Net Anatomy

In this chapter you will make a simple ball net. With this three dimensional object in hand it will be easier to examine its anatomy and relate the parts to the pattern diagrams. This ball net takes a 12 mm interior bead and can be used to make one of a pair of earrings or as a component of a necklace (see Chapter 7). However, since it is your first ball net you may want to keep it in your pattern box for later reference. For one ball net you will need:

Thread: 24 inches of size D Nymo or upholstery thread.
Needle: two thin but sturdy needles (John James #12 sharps)
Beads: four colors of size 10/0 and/or 11/0 beads with good sized holes. For purposes of illustration the instructions will refer to green, red, blue and yellow beads.
Other: one 12 mm bead of any material (an inexpensive one like plastic is suggested)

① Thread your needle. Put on a single seed bead and tie a simple knot around it about 6 inches from the end of your thread. This bead will serve as your "stop bead". It will be removed before the piece is finished so its color and size are immaterial. The portion of the thread that lies beyond the stop bead is the "tail thread". The portion of the thread on the other side of the stop bead, with the needle through it, is the "working thread".

② Put on 13 beads in the following color sequence: 2 green, 2 red, 1 yellow, 3 blue, 1 yellow, 2 red and 2 green. That is the first "down-column" of beads. Hold it with the tail thread at the top and the working thread coming out the bottom. With this orientation you will be able to follow the descriptions better.

③ Now pick up 2 green and 2 red beads and go through the bottom yellow bead to make a pear-shaped loop on the bottom of the work. This yellow bead is a "tie-in" bead. To make the loop, the thread goes through the yellow bead in the opposite direction than when the yellow bead was first put on in the down-column. In general, the second pass of a needle through a tie-in bead will be in the <u>opposite</u> direction from the first pass. All yellow beads in this piece are tie-in beads although that first one won't be tied-into until the end.

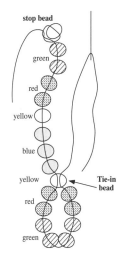

—— Ball Net for ——
12 mm Bead

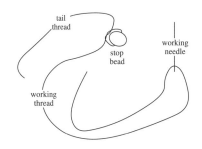

Threaded needle with a stop bead between tail and working threads. Length of tail and working threads will depend on intended use.

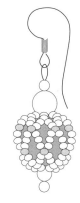

Pear-shaped loop at the bottom of the work made by going through the yellow tie-in bead in the opposite direction as when it was first put on in the down-column.

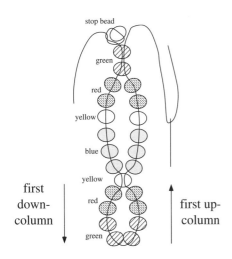

First down- and up-columns for a ball net that covers a 12 mm interior bead.

Now pick up 3 blue, 1 yellow, and 2 red and go through the top two green beads. Now you have one down- and one up-column. The picture is drawn with a lot of thread showing between the beads. This is for the purpose of illustration only and your piece should be very tight without any slack.

A new notation will now be introduced. The first down- and up-columns that you have just produced are presented below in a worded "bead chart". You read the left column of the bead chart from top to bottom and the right column, from bottom to top. A left-pointing arrow means that the thread ties-into the tie-in bead (yellow) or the spoke beads (green) at the same level in the previous column.

These bead charts will be used in all subsequent instructions to designate the sequence of beads and tie-ins. In the beginning of the book there will be three charts to describe each flat net. In Chapter 6 these will be combined into a single bead chart. Below is the first chart that describes the first down- and up-columns. You already know about tie-in beads and the meanings of the rest of terms in the middle column of the bead chart will be explained a bit later in the chapter.

1st down-column		1st up-column	
2 green	spoke top	<———	
2 red	cross piece	2	red
1 yellow	tie-in	1	yellow
3 blue	bridge span	3	blue
1 yellow	tie-in	<———	
2 red	cross piece	2	red
2 green	spoke bottom	2	green

④ Now repeat the up-column but in the down direction. In words: pick up 2 green and 2 red beads and go through the top yellow bead. Then put on 3 blue, 1 yellow, and 2 red beads and go through the bottom 2 green beads of the up-column. Notice that you tie-into the top yellow bead on the down-column and the bottom yellow bead on the up-column.

Below is the chart for the down-column you have just put on. Now put on the second up-column, going from the bottom to the top of the chart. Notice that the second up-column is identical to the first up-column.

Second down column is added to the ball net. Notice that the bottom tie-in bead is gone through with the up-column and the top tie-in bead is gone through with the second down-column.

2-5th down-column			2-5th up-column	
2	green	spoke top	<———	
2	red	cross piece	2	red
<———		tie-in	1	yellow
3	blue	bridge span	3	blue
1	yellow	tie-in	<———	
2	red	cross piece	2	red
<———		spoke bottom	2	green

5 Continue by adding 3 more down- and up-columns using the above bead chart until you have five columns of each type. The piece may be difficult to hold because it will want to curl up like a snail shell. Be patient - you are almost finished.

Add the sixth and last down-column. You should now have six spokes at the top of the net and six at the bottom. Your tail thread and stop bead are at the top left corner and your working thread is coming out the bottom spoke at the bottom right of the work. You are ready to "lace-up" with the last up-column. First, however, insert the 12 mm interior bead into the hollow of the beaded sphere. This will make the whole thing easier to hold. The bead chart below indicates what to do, but it will also be spelled out in words.

To start on the lace-up column, come up through the two green bottom spoke beads of the <u>first</u> down-column (bottom right-pointing arrow). Put on two red beads and tie-into the yellow tie-in bead on the 6th down-column (lower left-pointing arrow). Put on three blue beads and tie-into the yellow tie-in bead of the <u>first</u> down-column (upper right-pointing arrow). Put on two red beads and come up through the two green beads of the 6th down-column (top left-pointing arrow). In this and all future bead graphs, the <u>right</u> pointing arrows in the lace-up column indicate tie-ins to the spoke and tie-in beads of the <u>first</u> down-column. Flip over to the last page of this chapter for a graphical view of lacing up.

6th down-column			6th up-column	
2	green	spoke top	<———	
2	red	cross piece	2	red
<———		tie-in	——-——>	
3	blue	bridge span	3	blue
1	yellow	tie-in	<———-	
2	red	cross piece	2	red
<———-		spoke bottom	———->	

Tie off sequence in six steps. Only the top spoke, cross-piece and tie-in rows are shown.

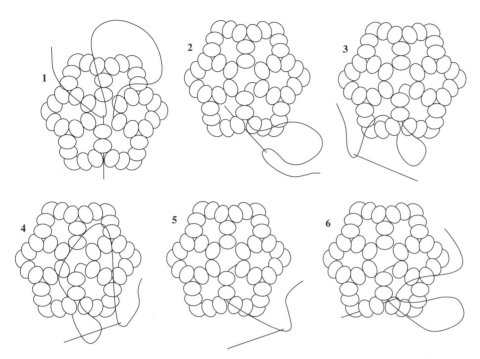

 Now you are ready to "tie off". Take off the stop bead and thread the second needle onto the 6 inches of tail thread. Take the tail needle with tail thread and go down through the top 2 green beads of the 6th down-column (1). Make a loop by passing the tail needle under the thread between the green and red bead (2-3), going through the loop (4) and pulling the thread tight for a single knot (5). You can make a second knot by going through the red beads (6) and tying a knot between the second red bead and the top yellow bead.

Now take your working needle and go through the top 2 green beads of the first down-column and tie off in the same manner as for the tail thread. Apply clear glue or nail polish to the knots and when dry, cut close to the knot. Or, if you used nylon thread, you can cut to 1/4 inch and burn the ends down carefully.

—— Net Anatomy ——

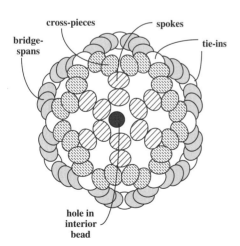

cross-pieces
spokes
bridge-spans
tie-ins
hole in interior bead

Top view of a ball net looking down through the hole in the interior bead.

Take a needle or pin and rotate the 12 mm interior bead so that the hole is surrounded by a ring of green beads. Looking down at the hole of the 12 mm bead, you should see a pleasing flower shape with the lines of beads forming the edges of six petals. Turn the covered bead over and the pattern should look the same. This net was described with four different colors of beads because each color represents a different part of the net.

The green beads are "spokes" like on a bicycle wheel that radiate out from the center or hub where the hole of the interior bead is located. The yellow beads are "tie-ins" since the needle goes through each of them twice. The red beads are "cross-pieces" and the blue beads form the "bridge-spans", in the sense that they connect the top half to the bottom half of the net.

Since a spherical net is a three-dimensional object it is difficult to represent it accurately in a two-dimensional diagram. The figures next to steps 3 and 4 are diagrams that show the sequence of beads and the way the thread ties them together. The bead charts are a shorthand way of presenting bead sequences in a particular pattern. A purely visual way of presenting the pattern is a "bead graph" which is easier to draw. Blank bead graphs for all patterns in this book are given in Appendix B. These may be duplicated as needed and colored for testing pattern ideas.

The bead graph shows the beads and threads for the ball net you have just finished. In the bead graph, the green spoke beads are drawn separated at the top (and bottom) where in reality they touch. The dotted thread lines that come out of the top of one column and go down the next column are shown loose, but in reality are as tight as they can be. In this manner any spherical net pattern can be graphed. Let us examine the parts of the graph while at the same time you relate the graph to your three dimensional ball net.

From top to bottom of the graph there are seven rows of bead segments. The top and bottom green segments are the spokes, as we learned earlier. They don't resemble spokes in this graph which is why they were introduced earlier. The second row of segments contains the red cross-pieces and the third, the yellow tie-ins. The fourth or middle row is the row of blue bridge-spans. Now go back to the three worded bead charts and see how these are designated in the middle column of each

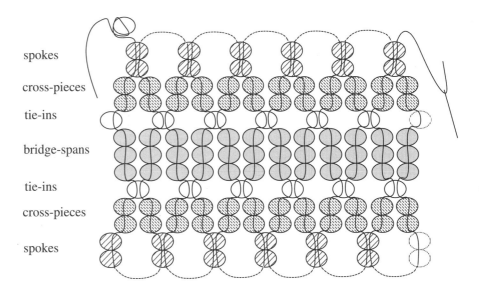

Bead graph for the six spoke ball net showing side view with spoke rows at bottom and top. Solid lines show path of thread from stop bead at upper left to working thread at upper right. Beads with dotted outline on right are tie-in beads on first down-column. Dotted arrows show thread path but are looser than in reality.

chart. Notice in the bead graph that there are six segments (counting from side to side) per spoke (green) row and six per tie-in (yellow) row. On the other hand, there are 12 segments in the crosspiece (red) rows and 12 in the bridge-span (blue) row. A general feature of all spherical nets is that there are twice as many segments in cross-piece and bridge-span rows as there are in spoke and tie-in rows. This makes sense since the thread goes through cross-pieces and bridge-spans only once whereas it passes through spokes and tie-ins two times each.

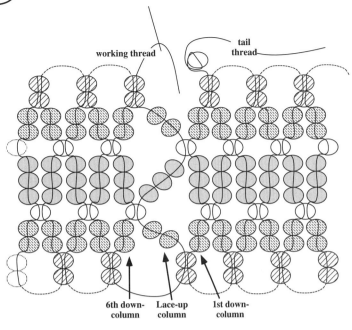

working thread

tail thread

6th down-column   Lace-up column   1st down-column

Modified bead graph to show the lace-up procedure. Only cross-piece and bridge-span rows are added in this step. Tie-ins and spokes are already in place in the last or first down-columns.

A bead graph also provides a way of visualizing the lace-up column. Most bead graphs will show the lace-up column on the far right edge of the piece. The bead graph below, however, has been redone to show the lace up column in the middle. You must use your imagination to mentally connect the right edge with the left edge of the piece and insert an interior bead. You start the lace-up column at the bottom by coming up through the two green bottom spoke beads on the first down-column. Put two red cross-piece beads on the needle and tie-into the yellow tie-in bead on the sixth down-column. Put on three blue beads and tie-into the yellow tie-in bead on the first down-column. Finally put on two red cross-piece beads and come up through the two green spoke beads on the sixth down column. Finish by tying off as described earlier.

As you will see in later chapters with other patterns, the number of spokes at the top and bottom can be increased or decreased according to need. Likewise the number of cross-piece rows can be any number with the following restriction: the number of cross-piece rows plus the number of bridge-span rows must be an odd number. In your first ball net this sum is three: two cross-piece rows and one bridge-span row. Some spherical net patterns don't have bridge-span rows: the baskets and bottle covers in Chapters 6 and 9 and the teardrop net in Chapter 7 are good examples. The teardrop net has five cross-piece rows and no bridge-span row but as you can see the sum (5 + 0) is still an odd number. The next rule dictates the number of tie-in rows. There will be one less tie-in row than there are cross-piece plus bridge-span rows. In your first ball net there are two tie-in rows. This follows from the fact that tie-in rows come between crosspiece and bridge-span rows. The last rule says that there are always exactly two spoke rows, one at the top and the other at the bottom of the piece.

It is not necessary to memorize these rules. They will come in handy, however, when you start to design your own spherical nets.

Nylon thread that comes on spools can be somewhat curly when you first unwind it. Some beaders wax their thread to make it straighter so it won't tangle as the piece is being constructed. Stretching the thread will also straighten it and you won't have the wax residue to contend with. To stretch a length of thread, wrap the end a couple of times around your index finger, unspool as much as you need and while holding the spool in your other hand, give it a couple of steady, healthy pulls. If the length you need is greater than 36 inches, you may need to stretch it in two or more steps.

3 Flat Nets and Anchoring

A flattened spherical net or "flat net" is constructed in much the same manner as the ball net in Chapter 2. The difference is that the flat net is laced up and tied off without inserting an interior bead. The empty net is then flattened into a disk so that the two spoke rows are right on top of each other in the center of the disk, with the bridge-span row at the edge. The top and bottom spoke rows are then tied together tightly or "anchored", which stabilizes the net into the flattened configuration. This anchoring together of the spoke rows is used in <u>many</u> spherical net patterns. It's not difficult to do, but it is a little hard to describe.

Before we get into flat nets and anchoring, a very important subject must be discussed. This subject is:

Tension is very important in constructing spherical nets. I didn't realize how important it was to emphasize tension until some friends, in order to help me with the text, made some of the pieces in the first chapters. Some of the trial pieces were pretty loose compared with the pieces I have made. My habits of keeping the nets tight were formed so long ago, that I had forgotten there were other ways to do stand-alone beadwork.

But tight tension is very important, especially for flat nets and baskets. These pieces do not have internal structures to dictate their shapes and rely on the internal tension between the beads and thread to keep their shapes. The larger the net, the more important the tension.

Keep your tension tight <u>as</u> you put on your down- and up-columns. It is next to impossible to take up slack from within a large piece. When you finish a column, pull the thread as tight as you can. Then hold the thread tight by looping the thread between your left-hand middle and ring fingers while you put on beads for the next step with your right hand. (If you are left handed, please reverse the hand directions.) Keep the tension as

—A Word on Tension—

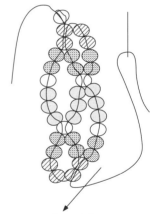

Keep your tension tight as you put on columns. When you finish a column, pull the thread as tight as you can.

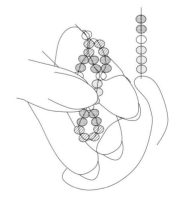

Hold the thread tight by looping the thread between your left-hand middle and ring fingers while you put on beads for the next step with your right hand.

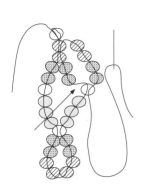 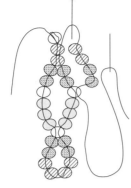 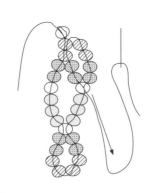

If you loose tension in the column just before the one you are workin on...

first go to the end of that column, pull it tight...

and then pull the current column tight.

you work up or down a column. If you loose tension in the column just before the one you are working on, go to the end of that column, pull it tight, hold the thread and then pull the current column tight.

How tight is tight enough? After you finish the third or fourth down- or up-column, pull the thread tight and hold the piece up at a 45 degree angle. Does it droop or does it stick straight out and not change shape no matter how you wave it back and forth. Can you make a net too tight? For large nets: no, the tighter the better. For small nets: well (I really hate to admit this but) yes. But only for the very smallest flat nets such as the top of the dangle earring in Chapter 5 and the top of the drop net earring in Chapter 7. You will know if a small flat net is too tight if you break a bead as you are tying off (assuming that the bead's hole is adaquate to accomodate the threads you are putting through it).

─How to Make a─ Flat Net Stay Flat

First we'll make another spherical net which will then be used to practice the anchoring steps for flat nets. This particular pattern is a part of several styles of earrings but for now you will use it to learn the flat net anchoring steps. For this project you will need:

Thread: 30 inches of size D Nymo or upholstery thread.

Needle: two thin but sturdy needles (John James #12 sharps)

Beads: four colors of size 10/0 and/or 11/0 beads with good sized holes. The pattern will be described using green, red, blue and yellow beads as before.

Other: a 4 or 5 mm faceted crystal or round bead for the center. A 5 mm bead will be too large to fit <u>into</u> the hole so it will ride on top, which is a nice effect. A 4 mm bead will fit inside the hole formed by the top row of spokes.

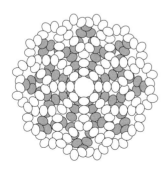

Top view of a small flat net with eight spokes. The bottom half of the net is shaded darker than the top.

There are eight spokes in this pattern instead of six as for the ball net in Chapter 2. The process of constructing the spherical net is described in bead charts in steps 1 through 4. The inclusion of the 4 or 5 mm center bead and the anchoring technique are described in steps 5 through 7. The bead graph for this flat net is shown in Appendix B.

1) Thread your needle and tie on a stop bead 6 inches from the end to form an 6-inch tail thread. Put on the first down- and up-columns following the chart below. Remember that the left-pointing arrows indicate tie-ins to the beads in the same level in the previous down- or up-column.

1st down-column			1st up-column	
3	green	spoke top	<———	
3	red	cross-piece	3	red
1	yellow	tie-in	1	yellow
3	blue	bridge span	3	blue
1	yellow	tie-in	<———	
3	red	cross-piece	3	red
3	green	spoke bottom	3	green

2) Now put on six more down- and up-columns following this chart until you have seven columns of each type.

2-7th down-column			2-7th up-column	
3	green	spoke top	<———	
3	red	cross-piece	3	red
<———		tie-in	1	yellow
3	blue	bridge span	3	blue
1	yellow	tie-in	<———	
3	red	cross-piece	3	red
<———		spoke bottom	3	green

3) Put on the last (eighth) down- and up-columns. The right-pointing arrows in the eighth up-column indicate tie-ins into the first down-column.

8th down-column			8th up-column	
3	green	spoke top	<———	
3	red	cross piece	3	red
<———		tie-in	———>	
3	blue	bridge span	3	blue
1	yellow	tie-in	<———	
3	red	cross piece	3	red
<———		spoke bottom	———>	

4) Take off the stop bead and thread a second needle onto the 6-inch tail thread. With the tail thread needle, go down through the top three green beads on the 8th down-column. Pull all slack out of the net and do a single tie off. Go through three red beads of one or the other cross-pieces and do a second tie off. Glue and cut close or cut and burn down. Take up your working needle and thread on the 4 or 5 mm center

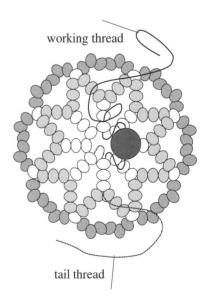

working thread

tail thread

View of the top of the net only showing the working thread coming out of the eighth spoke, through the center bead and through the first bead of the fourth spoke prior to tying off once. Tail comes out the top of the first spoke, down through three beads of the eighth spoke and is tied off.

bead. Then go through <u>only the first</u> green bead of the opposite spoke (4th spoke) so that the center bead lies over or just inside the hole formed by the 8 top spokes. Pull all the slack out and do a single tie off but don't cut the thread.

5 Squash the net flat so that holes formed by the top and bottom spoke rows are concentric, that is, the holes lie right on top of one another. The blue bridge-span beads will be at the edge of the two layered disk. Note that the green spoke beads in the bottom row lie <u>between</u> the green spoke beads in the top row. If they don't, flex the net around until they do.

Now we will concentrate on <u>anchoring</u> the top row of spokes to the bottom row of spokes. The figure shows two spoke rows in an "exploded view" as seen from the top without the center bead. The bottom spoke beads are shaded darker to make them distinguishable from the light top spoke beads. The working thread emerges from between the first and second green beads on the top fourth spoke row.

6 In the anchoring process you will weave your thread between the first and second beads of the spoke rows, from top to bottom to top, etc., all the way around the central space. Your thread will not go through the holes of any beads. Instead you will draw the thread under a bottom spoke and then over a top spoke pulling tight each time and popping your thread into the space <u>between</u> the first and second beads.

The figure has 16 "holes", labeled 1 through 16. The first hole is just to the right of where the working thread is tied off. With the working thread go down through hole number 1 and then up through hole number 2. Pull your thread tight. You may need to guide it with your thumb nail to get it to pop between the first and second beads of the bottom spoke row. Now put the needle down through hole number 3 and pull it tight, guiding the thread to pop between the first two green beads. Put the needle up through hole number 4 and pop the thread into place on the bottom spoke row. Continue around the center bead in a similar fashion until you bring the needle up through hole number 16. Put the needle down a second time through hole number 1 and pull tight.

Top view of the flat net showing only the three beads in the top (light) and bottom (dark) spoke rows. Beads are exploded outward to show the threads and holes between the first and second beads in each top and bottom spoke row.

7 Turn the flat net over so you can see what was the bottom spoke row during construction. Your working thread will emerge between two bottom row spokes. Insert the needle between the first and second bead of either spoke and go through the holes of the second and third green beads of that spoke toward the edge of the disk. You are virtually finished. Tie off the working thread, glue and cut short when dry. On the top of the flat net, finish tying off the tail thread if you have not already done so.

These figures show four steps in the anchoring process as seen from an edge-on view as if you could see between the first and second beads in the spoke rows. The working thread is tied off between the first and second beads of the top fourth spoke row. The top figure shows the working needle going down through the first hole. The second figure shows that the thread has been pulled tight and no longer shows above the top row of spokes. The needle is positioned to come back up through the second hole. The third figure shows the thread has been pulled tight after looping around the bottom spoke and is no longer visible from the bottom. The bottom figure shows the anchoring process has proceeded all the way around the center space and the needle is going back down the first hole, prior to tying off.

You may have had trouble getting your needle through the second and third spoke beads during the last tie off step. There are three possible reasons. First, your tension may have been so tight you had trouble getting your needle between the first and second beads. Tension is very important in making flat nets. For small flat nets like the one you just made, you may have to ease up a little during construction to facilitate tying off but not too much. On larger flat nets you will need to keep a tighter tension so the finished net is not too floppy.

An edge-on view of the anchoring process as if you could see between the first and second beads of each spoke.

Second, the holes in your green beads may be too small and won't easily admit a third pass of the needle, especially if you are using upholstery thread. If your problem in tying off was due to small-holed green beads, you need to use beads with larger holes. The size of the hole of the "second" position bead is critical. I have broken more than a few second position spoke beads in finishing off flat nets. It is frustrating to break a bead after all that work so take care to choose spoke beads with large enough holes.

A third possibility is that your needle is too flexible to force its way between the second and third spoke beads. This is why the 1.125 inch #12 needles (John James, Ltd.) are recommended for spherical net construction rather than the longer, more flexible "beading needles". My #12 sharps last a pretty long time, but they do get bent up and sometimes I break a needle trying to force it through a tight space. Usually, however, the needles I break have been used, abused and bent, and the metal has become fatigued. But this illustrates how much strength these needles are required to have to be useful in constructing spherical nets. If your needle has become bent, straighten it <u>very gently</u> with a pair of pliers.

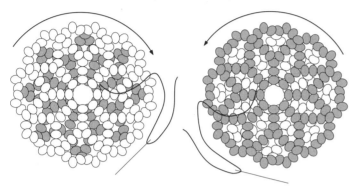

Clockwise on top or front.

Counter-clockwise on bottom or back.

The <u>anchoring</u> steps in Chapter 3 are described as proceeding in a <u>clockwise</u> fashion as seen from the top spoke rows. As you proceed around the center hole, you will need to turn the flat net over and view it from the bottom. The <u>apparent</u> direction you will be proceeding as seen from the bottom will be <u>counter-clockwise.</u> It is <u>very important</u> to understand this. Otherwise you will go around the same spoke again and again, rather than proceeding around the center bead. Actually it is quite arbitrary which direction you go as seen from the top as long as you proceed in the <u>opposite</u> direction as seen from the bottom. For myself I have set the rule that I always proceed clockwise on top and counter-clockwise on the bottom. This way I always know where I am and in what direction to proceed even if I come back to a piece after a long interlude. It is almost impossible to tell in which direction you are going by just looking at the piece. It is a lot easier to make a rule and stick to it.

4 Flat Nets with Ear Studs

Flat nets can be made into earrings ranging from 5/8 to 2 inches in diameter. Dangling earrings can be made by hanging flat nets by their bridge spans from ear hooks or earring findings for non-pierced ears that have loops for such purposes. Earring clips can be sewn to the backs of some flat nets to make non-pierced earrings that ride high on the ear lobe and are very comfortable. Clip earrings are discussed in detail in Chapter 8. The purpose of Chapter 4 is to demonstrate how to make flat nets into <u>stud</u> earrings for pierced ears.

Two styles of stud earrings are made out of flat nets: central and off-center ear studs. Flat nets with central studs are made by fitting a 4 mm cupped or a 6 mm flat ear stud behind the center bead just prior to the anchoring step detailed in Chapter 3. This process also requires that a soldered jump ring be incorporated in the bottom circle of spokes to ensure that the 4 mm cup or 6 mm flat ear stud does not come out. The incorporation of the soldered ring is the first subject of this chapter.

The second section will discuss using a 30 mm length of 20 gauge half-hard, gold-filled wire through the center bead to make an off-center stud. The off-center stud is preferred when the flat net has a diameter greater than 1.5 inches or 38 mm. This is because large disk earrings will flop over if there is too much mass above the stud compared with that below the stud. Small disk earrings (flat nets less than 1.5 inches) can have central studs because their small mass is held upright against the earlobe by the comfort clutch on the back of the lobe.

Central studs are made from commercially produced 4 mm cup or 6 mm flat stud findings. These studs are intended to be glued to a small bead or other object so the post part is relatively short. When incorporated into flat nets, the post that sticks out the back is barely long enough to catch the comfort clutch. People with thick earlobes may find that the 4 mm cup or 6 mm flat studs are simply not long enough. Nevertheless, the 4 mm cup or 6 mm flat stud makes a superior base for fringed earrings which are detailed in Chapter 5.

A soldered jump ring is incorporated into the bottom circle of spokes so that the cup or flat stud will not fall out. This requires

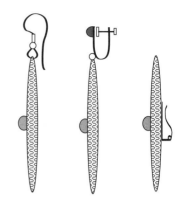

Flat nets can be made into earrings by attaching hooks or clips to the rim or sewing a clip back onto the back.

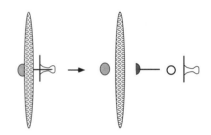

Flat net made into a central stud earring. A soldered jump ring is incorporated into the bottom row of spokes of the flat net and serves to hold the 4 mm cup or 6 mm flat stud in place behind the 4-5 mm center bead. The earring is held upright on the ear by a comfort clutch.

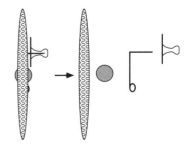

Flat net made into an off-center stud earring. The stud is made from a 36 mm length of 20 gauge half-hard gold-filled wire and goes through the 6 mm center bead. The earring is held upright on the ear by a comfort clutch.

that the jump ring be just the right size. It should be small enough that the base of the stud cannot pass through it and large enough that eight seed beads fit around the outside without crowding. The best I have found measure 4 mm or 5/36 inches on their outer diameter (OD) (see Appendix A: Sources of Supplies). Sometimes you can find jump rings that are already soldered. Since they are not visible from the front of the flat net, however, it is usually easier and cheaper to solder your own. Commercially purchased jump rings are recommended if you use them in any quantity since they are not easy to make from plain wire.

Soldered Jump Rings

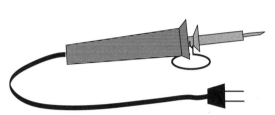

A soldering iron can be purchased from any hardware store. A small one with a small tip is preferred.

Top and side view of a stand for a soldering iron. One can be made from a 6-7 inch piece of 16-20 gauge wire. The base is 1.5 inches in diameter.

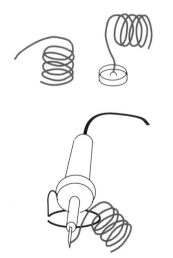

A coil of solid solder is dipped into the drop of flux before being melted onto the tip of the hot soldering iron.

A plain soldering iron, available in any hardware store, will do fine. Get one with a little wire stand, if possible, or make one in the shape shown. The best solder is Stay-brite by J.W. Harris Co. (Cincinnati, OH) which is available in jeweler supply stores (also see Appendix A). The silver solder kit contains half an ounce of silver solder and half an ounce of flux and will last forever.

First of all, position your soldering iron in its metal stand so that the tip is not touching anything and plug it in to let it heat up. Separate the jump rings to be soldered and close each one so that the opening is as small as possible. Get a little cup of water and position it near the soldering iron. Place a single drop of flux in the upturned cap of the soldering kit. When the iron is hot, dip the end of the coil of solder into the flux and melt a drop of solder onto the tip of the iron. It will stay molten as long as the iron is hot. (Old soldering irons may have deposits built up on the tip that prevent them from getting very hot and make it difficult to melt a drop of solder on them. Encrusted tips can be cleaned with a wire brush also available in hardware stores.)

Now pick up a jump ring with a pair of tweezers on the side of the ring opposite the opening. Dip the opening of the ring in the drop of flux - a little will flow into the opening. Then barely touch the ring opening to the drop of solder on the iron. The solder should flow onto the ring and into the opening. Immediately drop the ring into the cup of water to cool it. Proceed to the remaining jump rings.

When all the jump rings have been soldered, unplug the iron and leave it in its stand until completely cool. If any solder remains on the tip, leave it since it can be used next time. Dry off your soldered rings and store in a ziplock bag. If any of your rings have sharp or thick projections of solder, smooth them down with a diamond nail file or fine grit (200 - 400) carbide sandpaper.

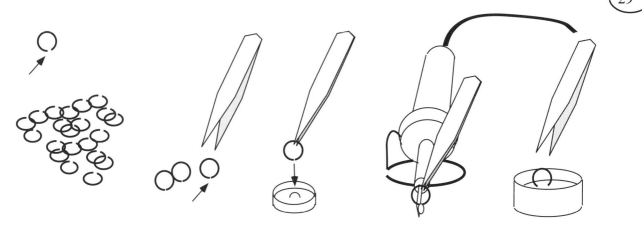

Sequence of steps for making soldered jump rings. Close each ring with pliers, pick one up on the side opposite the opening, dip opening in flux, touch opening to the solder, and drop immediately in water. Repeat for each jump ring.

The flat net used in this lesson is the same as that used in Chapter 3. The color pattern is being repeated because of the need to concentrate on the inclusion of the soldered ring. More esthetically pleasing color patterns can be found in Chapter 8. For this flat net you will need:

—Central Stud Flat—
Net Earrings

Thread: 30 inches of size D Nymo or upholstery thread.

Needle: two thin but sturdy needles (John James #12 sharps)

Beads: four colors of size 10/0 and/or 11/0 beads with good sized holes. The pattern will be described using green, red, blue and yellow beads as before.

Other: a 4 or 5 mm faceted crystal or round bead for the center. One soldered ring with an outer diameter of 4 mm or 5/32 inches. One 4 mm cup or 6 mm flat ear stud.

① Thread your needle and put on a stop bead, leaving a 6 inch tail thread. Put on the following sequence of beads for the first down- and up-columns. Put on the soldered ring before starting on the up column but let it float free in the loop formed between the two bottom spokes.

Exploded view of a flat net with a central stud showing various components. The stud shown here is a 4 mm cup stud but a 6 mm flat stud can also be used.

1st down-column		1st up-column	
3	green	spoke top	<———-
3	red	cross piece	3 red
1	yellow	tie-in	1 yellow
3	blue	bridge span	3 blue
1	yellow	tie-in	<———-
3	red	cross piece	3 red
3	green	spoke bottom	3 green
		soldered ring	

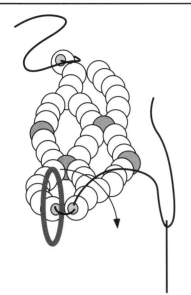

Looking from the bottom at the net with two down- and one up-columns. The soldered ring is rotated one quarter turn to the right.

(2) Put on the beads in the second <u>down column only</u> in the next chart. Hold the piece in your left hand and pull the soldered ring between the two green spokes so it touches the thread. Grip the beads with the left hand; and with the right, rotate the ring 90° (one quarter of a circle) to the right. Hold the ring in this position. Take up the needle in your right hand and pass it <u>down</u> through the ring and take up any slack in your thread. <u>Now</u> put on the beads in the second up-column.

2-7th down-column			2-7th up-column	
3	green	spoke top	<————	
3	red	cross piece	3	red
<————		tie-in	1	yellow
3	blue	bridge span	3	blue
1	yellow	tie-in	<————	
3	red	cross piece	3	red
<————		spoke bottom	3	green
		soldered ring		

The soldered ring is rotated one quarter turn to the right and the needle is passed down through the ring prior to putting on the second up-column.

(3) Repeat the down- and up-columns in Step 2 for the third through seventh down- and up-columns. Be sure to go <u>down</u> through the soldered ring after you come out of the bottom spoke beads on each down-column.

(4) To finish off, put on the following sequence for the eighth down- and eighth or lace-up-column. As before, go <u>down</u> through the soldered ring before coming back up through the bottom spoke beads on the first down-column.

8th down-column			8th up-column	
3	green	spoke top	<————	
3	red	cross piece	3	red
<————		tie-in	————->	
3	blue	bridge span	3	blue
1	yellow	tie-in	<————	
3	red	cross piece	3	red
<————		spoke bottom	————->	
		soldered ring		

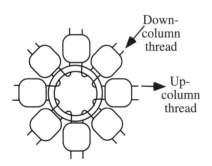

Down-column thread

Up-column thread

A jump ring with eight green bottom spoke beads neatly encircling it. Each thread comes out a spoke bead and over the ring before entering the bead to the right.

(5) Take the stop bead off the tail thread and thread on the second needle. With the tail needle go down through the top three green beads of the eighth down-column and tie off. Go through two red beads of one of the cross-pieces and tie off a second time. Glue and cut close when dry or cut and burn down carefully. With the working thread, put on a 4 or 5 mm center bead and go down through the first green bead of the fourth spoke, exactly opposite the eighth spoke. Tie off once.

6 With a pair of tweezers or chain nosed pliers, pick up the 4 mm cup or 6 mm flat stud by the rim. Pass it stem first through an opening in the side of the net and guide the stem out through the soldered ring. Flatten the net, making sure the stud doesn't fall out and that the cup or pad rests behind the 4-5 mm center bead. A 4 mm cup stud will wobble since it is not attached to the ring but merely "captured" by it. A 6 mm flat stud won't wobble nearly as much. Using the working thread, anchor the top ring of spokes to the bottom ring as described in Chapter 3. Tie off.

Pick up the 4 or 6 mm stud by the rim and insert stem-first through the side of the net, and out through the soldered ring, trapping the cup or pad behind the center bead.

In making small flat net stud earrings with eight spokes, you must first decide on which type of stud to use: a 4 mm cup stud, a 6 mm flat stud or an off-center stud. No method of construction is perfect so it might be useful to consider the advantages and disadvantages of each.

4 mm cup stud
Advantages:
    edges of cup don't cut anchor thread
Disadvantages:
    wobbles
    needs soldered ring
    studs may be difficult to find
    post is relatively short

off-center wire stud
Advantages:
    doesn't need soldered ring
    post can be made longer
Disadvantages:
    moves back and forth
    makes dangle earrings hang low

6 mm flat stud
Advantages:
    doesn't wobble
    studs are easier to find
Disadvantages:
    edges may cut anchor thread
    needs soldered ring
    post is relatively short

The off-center stud earring has 10 spokes on the top and bottom which surround a 6 mm center bead. The construction of the flat net is similar to the one described in Chapter 3, only this one will have more beads per column so the final diameter is just over 1.5 inches. The pattern is described with same four colors of beads used previously. The bead graph is in Appendix B. For one earring you will need:

Thread: 45 inches of size D Nymo or upholstery thread.

Needle: two thin but sturdy needles (John James #12 sharps)

Beads: four colors of size 10/0 and/or 11/0 beads with good sized holes. The pattern will be described using green, red, blue and yellow beads as before.

Other: a 6 mm faceted crystal or round bead for the center. One 30 mm (1 3/16 inch) length of 20 gauge, half-hard, gold-filled wire.

— Off-Center Stud — Earrings

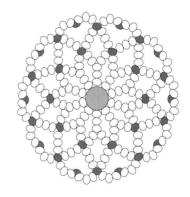

Top view of a ten spoke flat net with a 6 mm center bead and off center stud. Only the top of the flat net is shown.

1 Thread your needle and put on a stop bead, leaving 6 inches of thread in the tail. Put on the following down- and up-columns:

1st down-column			1st up-column	
3	green	spoke top	<———	
2	red	cross piece	2	red
1	yellow	tie-in	1	yellow
3	red	cross piece	3	red
1	yellow	tie-in	<———	
3	blue	bridge span	3	blue
1	yellow	tie-in	1	yellow
3	red	cross piece	3	red
1	yellow	tie-in	<———	
2	red	cross piece	2	red
3	green	spoke bottom	3	green

2 Put on the second through ninth down- and up-columns.

2-9th down-column			2-9th up-column	
3	green	spoke top	<———	
2	red	cross piece	2	red
<———		tie-in	1	yellow
3	red	cross piece	3	red
1	yellow	tie-in	<———	
3	blue	bridge span	3	blue
<———		tie-in	1	yellow
3	red	cross piece	3	red
1	yellow	tie-in	<———	
2	red	cross piece	2	red
<———		spoke bottom	3	green

3 Put on the tenth down-column and the tenth or lace-up up-column.

10th down-column			10th up-column	
3	green	spoke top	<———	
2	red	cross piece	2	red
<———		tie-in	———>	
3	red	cross piece	3	red
1	yellow	tie-in	<———	
3	blue	bridge span	3	blue
<———		tie-in	———>	
3	red	cross piece	3	red
1	yellow	tie-in	<———	
2	red	cross piece	2	red
<———		spoke bottom	———>	

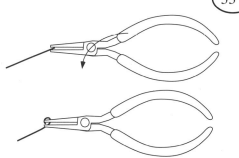

4 Take off the stop bead and thread the second needle onto the tail thread. Using the tail needle go through the top three spoke beads on the tenth down-column. Tie off once. Using the working needle, go through only the first bead on the first down-column and tie off once.

5 Take the 30 mm length of 20 gauge, half-hard, gold-filled (or silver) wire. Using your 200-400 grit carbide sandpaper, smooth off each end by rubbing in a circular motion. Test the end against the skin of the back of your hand. If it feels sharp or rough, sand it some more until it feels fairly smooth.

Grip the wire at the very tip with a pair of round nosed pliers. Rotate the pliers three-fourths of a circle counter-clockwise to form a small loop in the wire.

With a pair of round-nosed pliers, make a small loop at one end of the wire. Put the 6 mm center bead into the interior of the net and flatten the net with your fingers so that the 6 mm bead is in the center between the top and bottom spokes. Hold the flattened net so that you can see the top spokes where the working and tail threads are tied. Take the ear wire and stick the straight end between two top spokes, through the hole of the 6 mm center bead and out between two spokes on the opposite side of the disk where it went in. Make sure there are five spokes on either side of the wire. Try to position the ear wire away from the spokes where the working and tail threads are tied.

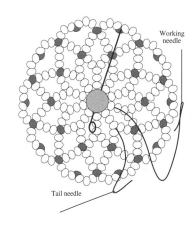

6 Using the working thread, anchor the top spokes to the bottom spokes as described in chapter 3. Go all the way around the center bead and tie off your working thread on the same side of the disk that you tied off the tail thread. Tie off each thread again if you wish. Glue and clip close when dry.

Above, ten spoke flat net with a 6 mm center bead just prior to anchoring with the working thread. Below, the finished earring with the ear wire bent at a right angle to the flat net. Loop in the wire is pulled snugly against the center bead.

Pull the wire so that the loop is snug against the 6 mm center bead. With a pair of needle nose pliers, bend the ear wire at a right angle to the plane of the disk 9 mm from the tip opposite the loop. In the anchoring process for the off-center stud, you should notice that the ear wire is <u>between</u> spokes on back side, but directly <u>behind</u> spokes on the front. Because of this, the anchoring process is not very much different from the basic method described in Chapter 3.

Edge-on view of the anchoring process as if you could see between the first and second beads of each spoke. Compare this figure with that in Chapter 3.

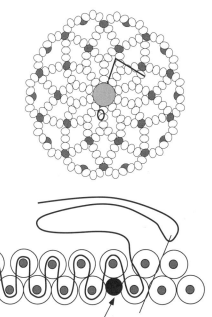

Front Spokes

Back Spokes

Earwire lying between back spokes and behind front spokes

One difference should be noted, however. In Chapter 3 and in the first half of this Chapter, the "top" spokes of the spherical net became the "front" of the earring. In patterns with off center ear studs, the "top" of the spherical net becomes the "back" of the disk of the earring.

—A Short Note on—
Seed Beads

tall and
narrow

short
and wide

Seed beads are not all the same shape or size. Even seed beads that are said to be of a single size, such as 11/0, are quite variable. If a bead is stood on its end, with its hole vertical, then it can be classified as either tall and narrow or short and wide... or anything in between.

For central-stud earrings, the beads in the first position on the bottom spoke, i.e. on the edge of the bottom circle, should be narrow so eight of them will fit around the soldered ring. It may take some trial and error to know which of your beads are narrow enough. The Japanese 11/0 beads are usually ok but use the narrowest ones in the batch.

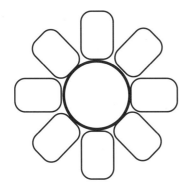

Narrow beads fit nicely around the soldered ring on the bottom of a central stud earring.

Seed beads used in spherical nets should have good sized holes. Most Japanese seed beads have relatively large holes and I have had little trouble using them as spoke beads through which the needle passes up to three times. Size D Nymo thread is thinner than upholstery thread. It is a lot easier to get through the eye of #12 needles and through small holed beads. Unfortunately, D Nymo is sometimes difficult to find in colors whereas upholstery thread is available in almost all fabric stores.

Czech 9/0 3-cut seed beads are often quite variable, especially older beads. They can vary as much as threefold as measured by the length of their holes although their width is fairly uniform. I like these beads because of their large holes. I try, however, to use the same size bead in a single position. They do not do well in the first spoke position around the soldered ring because they are too wide.

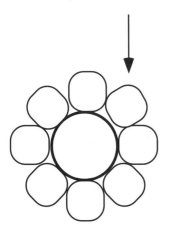

Wider beads crowd around the soldered ring on the bottom of a central stud earring, resulting in one bead being forced away from the ring.

Czech and Japanese 11/0 2-cut beads are usually rather narrow and eight of them will fit comfortably around a soldered ring for the central stud earrings. I don't care for them as much, however, in the body of the flat net.

5 Fringes for Earrings and Pins

Earrings with fringes are very popular and flat nets are excellent bases for fringed earrings. In this chapter you will learn how fringes can be attached to flat nets to make earrings and pins. Two patterns will be presented in detail: the first is an earring with a central stud, as described in Chapter 4, and with nine dangles. The second is a two inch flat net pin with 17 dangles. This lesson also introduces the use of an off-center stud as a pinning mechanism that is secured with a tie-tack back or "keeper".

This earring is constructed in two pieces using different needles and possibly different threads. The flat net base needs a strong nylon while the fringe needs a more delicate one so it will hang nicely. For one base you will need:

Thread: 24 inches of size D Nymo or upholstery thread.

Needle: two thin but sturdy needles (John James #12 sharps)

Beads: two colors of size 10/0 and/or 11/0 beads with good sized holes. The instructions will refer to green and pink beads.

Other: a 4 or 5 mm faceted crystal or round bead for the center. One soldered ring with an outer diameter of 4 mm or 5/32 inches. One 4 mm cup or 6 mm flat ear stud. One comfort clutch.

① Thread your needle and put on a stop bead leaving about 6 inches in your tail thread. Put on the left column of beads for your first down-column. Be sure to put on the soldered ring prior to starting on the right up-column. You may want to review how to incorporate a soldered ring into a flat net in Chapter 4.

1st down-column			1st up-column	
3	green	spoke top	<———	
2	pink	cross piece	2	pink
1	green	tie-in	1	green
2	green	bridge span	2	green
1	green	tie-in	<———	
2	pink	cross piece	2	pink
3	green	spoke bottom	3	green
	soldered ring			

——Earrings with —— Fringes

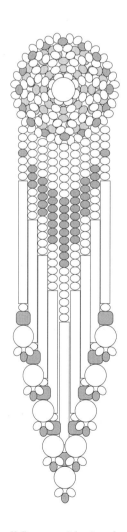

Small flat net with nine dangles.

2 For the second through seventh down- and up-columns use the following:

2-7th down-column		2-7th up-column
3 green	spoke top	<———
2 pink	cross piece	2 pink
<———	tie-in	1 green
2 green	bridge span	2 green
1 green	tie-in	<———
2 pink	cross piece	2 pink
<———	spoke bottom	3 green
down thru	**soldered ring**	

3 Finish the flat net by putting on the eighth down-column and the eighth or lace-up up-column.

8th down-column		8th up-column
3 green	spoke top	<———
2 pink	cross piece	2 pink
<———	tie-in	———>
2 green	bridge span	2 green
1 green	tie-in	<———
2 pink	cross piece	2 pink
<———	spoke bottom	———>
down thru	**soldered ring**	

4 Finish the flat net earring base by taking off the stop bead and threading the second needle onto the tail thread. Pass the tail needle down through the first three green beads on the eighth down-column and tie off. Using the working needle, put on the 4 or 5 mm center bead and go through the first bead on the fourth down-column and tie off. Insert a 4 mm cup or 6 mm flat stud into the net and extend the pointed end out through the soldered jump ring with the cup or pad nesting behind the center bead. Anchor the top spoke row to the bottom one as described in Chapter 3. Tie off both the working and tail threads and glue and cut when dry or burn down carefully.

Bugle beads come in a variety of lengths from 5 to 35 mm. Sometimes, however, you may not have the size of bugle bead you need. Bugle beads of shorter length can be made from longer ones or from broken bugles. To cut a bugle bead, lay the bead along a ruler and score it by dragging an edge of a triangular file at a right angle to the bugle bead at the desired length. Pick up the bead and apply gentle pressure to the side opposite the scoring until the bead snaps in two. If the scoring mark is close to one end, use a pair of pliers to grip that end. Smooth the cut edge by rubbing it against your square of carbide sandpaper.

Now you are ready to attach the fringe. For the fringe on one earring you will need:

Thread: 60 inches of size B or D Nymo thread.

Needle: a thin long needle (Best Quality Beading Needles #13)

Beads: two colors of size 10/0 and/or 11/0 beads with good sized holes. The instructions will refer to green and pink beads.

Other: nine 4 or 5 mm green beads of stone or glass - same ones you used as a center bead for the flat net, nine green 20-25 mm bugle beads, and nine pink seed beads of size 6/0 - 8/0, also known as "pony" beads.

Hold the flat net vertically with the front facing you so that you see the pattern at the right. The hole in the center bead will not be either horizontal nor vertical. One of the front tie-in beads should be exactly at the bottom. It doesn't matter which one. This will be the location of the middle dangle, number 5 in the table below. Since I am right handed, I put my dangles on from right to left. I have numbered the dangles in the table to refect this directionality, but since the fringe is side-to-side symmetrical, it can be read either way.

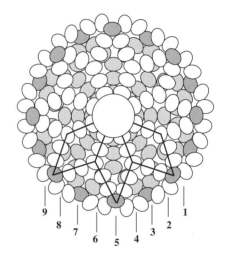

Flat net for earring with fringe showing position of each dangle. The three diamond shapes are superimposed to show three front tie-ins.

The first dangle will be directly below the front tie-in bead to the right of the central one and the ninth dangle is below the front tie-in to the left. The even numbered dangles (2, 4, 6, and 8) are between the two beads in the bridge-spans and the 3rd and 7th are below the back tie-in beads just to either side of the central front tie-in.

Dangle#	9	8	7	6	5	4	3	2	1
Beads	f	c	b	c	f	c	b	c	f
green	3	4	5	6	7	6	5	4	3
pink	1	3	5	7	9	7	5	3	1
green	3	4	5	6	7	6	5	4	3
bugle	1	1	1	1	1	1	1	1	1
green	1	1	1	1	1	1	1	1	1
pony	1	1	1	1	1	1	1	1	1
4-5mm	1	1	1	1	1	1	1	1	1
triplet	1	1	1	1	1	1	1	1	1

The green and pink colors refer to seed beads. The "triplet" is a set of three turn-around beads under the 4-5 mm bead. A green-pink-green sequence is suggested. Letters f, b and c refer to the position on the flat net under which each dangle is located: f for front tie-in, b for back tie-in and c for center of bridge-span.

The "triplet" is a set of three beads below the 4-5 mm bead on the bottom of a dangle. The thread goes through the triplet only once while it goes through the rest of the beads on the dangle twice.

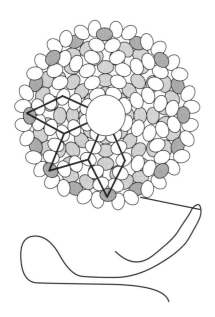

Insert needle through two bridge-span beads just to the right of the front tie-in bead where the first dangle hangs.

(5) To start the fringe, thread your needle with the Nymo thread. From right to left, go through the two bridge-span beads just to the right of the front tie-in bead where the first dangle hangs. Leave about 3 inches of Nymo thread exposed and with your fingers, guide it around the flat net thread and tie a single knot. Pick up the fringe needle and gently pull the thread tight. This will pull the knot you just tied through the two bridge-span beads.

(6) Put on the beads in the first dangle including the triplet at the bottom. Go back up through the 4-5 mm bead and the rest of beads in the first dangle. Go through the first bead in the bridge span just to the left. Adjust the tension to be snug but not stiff. Put on the beads in the next dangle, come back up and go through the second bead in the bridge-span to the left. Adjust the tension.

(7) Continue with the third through ninth dangle, advancing a single bead in the bridge-span each time. After the ninth dangle, go through the two beads in the bridge-span to the left, tie off once, go through the tie-in bead on the flat net and tie off again.

Put a needle on the tail thread to the right of the first dangle. Go through the tie-in bead on the flat net and tie off once. Glue each final knot and cut close when dry or burn down carefully.

You're done. Now make another one just like it and you have a pair. Enjoy.

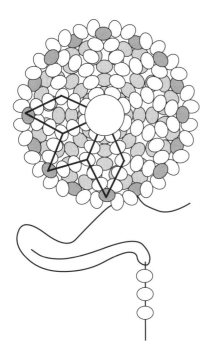

Leave a 3 inch tail and with your fingers loop the tail thread around the flat net thread and tie a single knot. Pull the knot through the two bridge-span beads before putting on the beads for the first dangle.

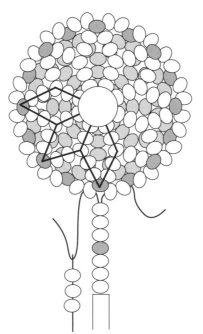

Put on the beads of the first dangle including the three beads in the triplet at the bottom. Come back up through the 4-5 mm bead and the rest of the dangle. Then go through the first bead of the bridge-span to the left.

This is a 2 inch flat net with 17 dangles. The pin mechanism is similar to the off-center stud earring and is held in place with a tie-tack back or keeper. The tie-tack back needs one inch of 18 gauge brass or nickel wire that is sharpened on one end. The pin will be done in two stages: the flat net base and then the fringe. The bead graph for the flat net base is in Appendix B. For the flat net base you will need:

Thread: 72 inches of size D Nymo or upholstery thread.

Needle: two thin but sturdy needles (John James #12 sharps)

Beads: two colors of size 10/0 and/or 11/0 beads with good sized holes. The instructions will refer to green and pink beads.

Other: 1 inch of 18 gauge brass or nickel wire, one 8 mm green bead of stone or glass for center bead (make sure the 18 gauge wire can go through the center), and one tie-tack back (make sure the tie-tack back will grip the 18 gauge wire).

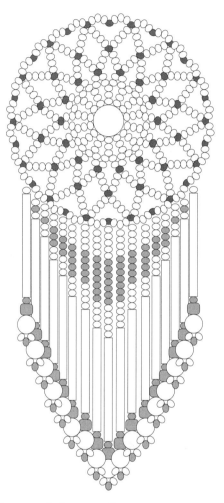

A two inch diameter flat net serves as a base for a pin with 17 dangles. Only the front half of the flat net is shown.

5 Thread your needle and put on a stop bead, leaving about six inches of tail thread. Make the first down- and up-columns.

1st down-column			1st up-column	
3	green	spoke top	<———	
2	green	cross piece	2	green
1	pink	tie-in	1	pink
3	pink	cross piece	3	pink
1	pink	tie-in	<———	
4	green	cross piece	4	green
1	green	tie-in	1	green
3	pink	bridge-span	3	pink
1	green	tie-in	<———	
4	green	cross piece	4	green
1	pink	tie-in	1	pink
3	pink	cross piece	3	pink
1	pink	tie-in	<———	
2	green	cross piece	2	green
3	green	spoke bottom	3	green

72 inches is the longest thread length that is recommended. This is double my arm length and so is the most I can pull through a tie-in bead in a single motion. If you have shorter arms you might find it more comfortable to work with shorter lengths of thread.

2 Make the second through 13th down- and up-columns.

2-13th down-column			2-13th up-column	
3	green	spoke top	<———	
2	green	cross piece	2	green
<———		tie-in	1	pink
3	pink	cross piece	3	pink
1	pink	tie-in	<———	
4	green	cross piece	4	green
<———		tie-in	1	green
3	pink	bridge-span	3	pink
1	green	tie-in	<———	
4	green	cross piece	4	green
<———		tie-in	1	pink
3	pink	cross piece	3	pink
1	pink	tie-in	<———	
2	green	cross piece	2	green
<———		spoke bottom	3	green

3 Make the fourteenth down- and up-columns.

14th down-column			14th up-column	
3	green	spoke top	<———	
2	green	cross piece	2	green
<———		tie-in	———>	
3	pink	cross piece	3	pink
1	pink	tie-in	<———	
4	green	cross piece	4	green
<———		tie-in	———>	
3	pink	bridge-span	3	pink
1	green	tie-in	<———	
4	green	cross piece	4	green
<———		tie-in	———>	
3	pink	cross piece	3	pink
1	pink	tie-in	<———	
2	green	cross piece	2	green
<———		spoke bottom	———>	

4 Take off the stop bead and thread a second needle onto the tail thread. With the tail needle, go through the top three beads of the 14th down column and tie off once. With the working needle, go through the first bead of the first down column and tie off once.

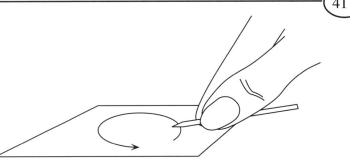

5 Sharpen the 1 inch length of 18 gauge wire. You can do this using your piece of 200-400 grit carbide sandpaper. Holding the wire nearly parallel to the sandpaper, rub in a circular motion while slowly rotating the wire. Test for sharpness by sticking the wire through a piece of tightly woven or knitted material. Once it is sharp enough, polish the end with a rouge cloth. If you have a grinding wheel and buffer, all the better. Make a small loop on the non-sharpened end with a pair of round nosed pliers.

6 Put the 8 mm bead into the interior of the net through the hole made by the 14 spokes at the top or bottom of the net. Squish the net flat, while keeping the 8 mm bead in the holes made by the spokes. Hold the net so that you are looking at the side with the tail and working threads (this will be the back side). Stick the pointy end of the wire between two spokes, through the hole in the 8 mm bead and out between two spokes opposite the entry point. Count to make sure there are 7 spokes on either side of the wire. Hold the net flat with the fingers of your left hand. The threads with your needles attached are tied off on spokes 1 and 14. It is best if your wire goes in between spokes 10 and 11 and comes out between spokes 3 and 4. This is just a suggestion. The main point is to keep the tie off procedures away from the wire to reduce confusion.

7 Holding the net flat in your left hand while keeping the 8 mm bead in the center and the wire in place, anchor the net using the working thread as described in Chapter 3. Come all the way around the circle of spokes. After you bring the needle up between the 14th and 1st spokes, insert the needle through the second and third beads in the first spoke and tie off. Go through the two pink beads in the top cross-piece and tie off a second time. Do the same with the tail thread. Apply glue and cut close when dry or burn down carefully. With a pair of needle or chain nosed pliers, bend the wire 90° about 9 mm from the pointy end.

For the fringe you will need:

Thread: two 54 inch lengths of size B or D Nymo thread.

Needle: a thin long needle (Best Quality Beading Needles #13)

Beads: two colors of size 10/0 and/or 11/0 beads with good sized holes. The instructions will refer to green and pink beads.

Other: 17 green beads of 4 or 5 mm diameter of stone or glass, similar to the ones you used as a center bead for the flat net but smaller, 17 green 30 mm bugle beads and 17 pink seed beads of size 6/0 - 8/0, also known as "pony" beads.

Orientation of the center bead with pointy end at the top and loop at the bottom. Wire is at the back and not seen from this view.

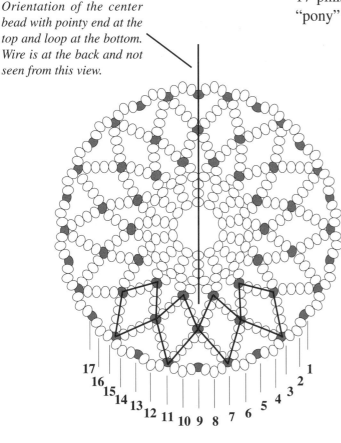

Hold the flat net so that you are looking at the front with the wire through the center bead in a vertical orientation (remember that the wire sticks out on the back). The loop should be at the bottom and the pointy end at the top. Trace the path of the wire down to the edge of the flat net. The last bead directly below the loop of the wire is a tie-in bead on <u>back</u> side of the flat net. This will be the location of the central dangle which is number 9 in the fringe chart below. The location of the first dangle is below the second back tie-in bead to the right. The seventeenth dangle is below the second back tie-in bead to the left of the central one. This is different from the earring described earlier in this Chapter, where the central dangle was below a <u>front</u> tie-in bead.

Flat net base for the pin showing positions of each dangle. Only the front of the net is shown. The four diamond shapes are superimposed on the flat net to aid in locating the positions of the dangles.

Dangle#	17	16	15	14	13	12	11	10	9	8	7	6	5	4	3	2	1
Beads	b	c	f	c	b	c	f	c	b	c	f	c	b	c	f	c	b
green	1	1	2	2	3	3	4	4	5	4	4	3	3	2	2	1	1
pink	0	1	1	3	3	5	5	7	7	7	5	5	3	3	1	1	0
green	0	1	2	2	3	3	4	4	5	4	4	3	3	2	2	1	0
bugle	1	1	1	1	1	1	1	1	1	1	1	1	1	1	1	1	1
green	1	1	1	1	1	1	1	1	1	1	1	1	1	1	1	1	1
pony	1	1	1	1	1	1	1	1	1	1	1	1	1	1	1	1	1
4-5mm	1	1	1	1	1	1	1	1	1	1	1	1	1	1	1	1	1
triplet	1	1	1	1	1	1	1	1	1	1	1	1	1	1	1	1	1

The green and pink colors refer to seed beads. The "triplet" is a set of three turn-around beads under the 4-5 mm bead. A green-pink-green sequence is suggested. Letters f, b and c refer to the position on the flat net under which each dangle is located: f for front tie-in, b for back tie-in and c for center of bridge-span.

8 Thread the #13 needle with 72 inches of Nymo thread. Hold the net flat in your left hand, front side facing you. Working from left to right, go through the three pink beads in the bridge-span that is fifth from the central tie-in, leaving a 4 inch tail sticking out. Using your fingers, loop the tail Nymo thread around the flat net thread and tie off once. Pull the knot forward through the bridge-span beads by grasping the working thread and pulling gently.

Check your position and compare it to the figure. Your thread should be directly below a back tie-in bead that is two <u>back</u> tie-in beads to the right of where the central dangle will be. There will also be two front tie-in beads between the first and central dangles. The even numbered dangles will fall below the central bead of each bridge-span.

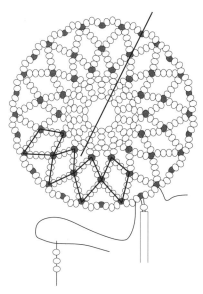

Go through the three pink beads in the bridge-span that is fifth from the central tie-in. Tie off the tail. Put on the beads in the first dangle and go through the first bead in the next bridge-span.

9 Put on the beads of the first dangle, including the triplet at the bottom. Come back up through the 4-5 mm bead and the rest of the beads in the dangle. Pull out the slack but don't tighten it to the point that the dangle is stiff.

10 Go through the first bead of the bridge-span to the left. Put on the beads of the second dangle and thread your way back up the column. <u>Skipping the central bead of the bridge-span</u>, go through the third bead from right to left.

11 Continue adding dangles from right to left. Odd numbered dangles will be under tie-in beads and even numbered ones, under the central bead in the bridge-spans. When your thread gets short, tie it off in the body of the flat net. Rethread your needle with the second 72 inch length of Nymo. Tie off somewhere in the flat net and work your way to the point in the fringe where you left off. Continue adding dangles.

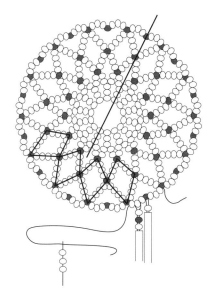

After putting on the beads in the second dangle and coming back through them, skip the middle bead in the bridge-span and go through the third bead. Continue with the third through 17th dangles.

12 After adding the 17th dangle, go through the three beads of the bridge-span to the left. Tie off once and go through the tie-in bead and tie off again. Glue and cut short when dry or burn down carefully. Thread a short needle onto your tail thread and tie off in a similar manner. You are finished.

6 Baskets and Bottle Covers

In this chapter you will learn to make a two-layered basket and a single-layered bottle cover. These are the largest flat nets you will learn to make from this book, but they are also relatively simple since there are no special attachments such as soldered rings. The real challenge is keeping the pattern straight. Baskets are merely large flat nets that you learned about in Chapter 3 and bottle covers are large ball nets from Chapter 2.

The basket pattern that will be used to demonstrate the technique is called a rimless basket. Two colors of beads will be used: a dark color for the exterior and a light color for the lining. Both colors of beads should have adequately sized holes. The dark color will serve as tie-in beads on the lining and the light colored beads will be tie-ins on the exterior. This will help you to find the tie-ins more easily and thereby decrease the chance of error.

The exterior and lining portions of the net are made together so that when you have finished the anchoring step, the basket is complete. This color scheme is very simple. Chapter 9 has some color schemes that make into really nice baskets. For the rimless basket you will need:

Thread: 3 or 4 lengths of size D Nymo or upholstery thread, each 72 inches long (cut as needed)

Needle: two thin but sturdy needles (John James #12 sharps)

Beads: two colors of size 10/0 and/or 11/0 beads with good sized holes. The instructions will refer to green and pink beads. Make sure you have at least one ounce (28 grams) of each. This is generous but it would be frustrating to run out.

Other: None

① Thread your needle and put on a stop bead, leaving a 6 inch tail thread. The bead charts presented in Chapters 2 through 5 have been combined and condensed into a single bead chart. Note the column designations at the top of the chart. The first and last columns are used only once but the middle two are used 17 times each. Be sure to keep a <u>really tight tension</u> especially during the 18th or lace-up column.

— Basket with — Lining

Rimless basket as seen from the side (about 3/4 scale). Individual beads are not shown but cross-piece sections are represented as solid lines that cross at the positions of the tie-in beads. A single layer of the exterior (darker lines) and of the lining (lighter lines) are shown.

Section	1st Dn		1-17th Up		2-18th Dn		18th Up	
Exterior								
spoke exterior	5	green	←———		5	green	←———	
cross piece	2	green	2	green	2	green	2	green
tie-in	1	pink	1	pink	←———		———→	
cross piece	3	green	3	green	3	green	3	green
tie-in	1	pink	←———		1	pink	←———	
cross piece	4	green	4	green	4	green	4	green
tie-in	1	pink	1	pink	←———		———→	
cross piece	5	green	5	green	5	green	5	green
tie-in	1	pink	←———		1	pink	←———	
cross piece	6	green	6	green	6	green	6	green
tie-in	1	pink	1	pink	←———		———→	
cross piece	5	green	5	green	5	green	5	green
tie-in	1	pink	←———		1	pink	←———	
cross piece	4	green	4	green	4	green	4	green
tie-in	1	pink	1	pink	←———		———→	
cross piece	3	green	3	green	3	green	3	green
tie-in	1	pink	←———		1	pink	←———	
cross piece	2	green	2	green	2	green	2	green
tie-in	1	pink	1	pink	←———		———→	
Lining								
cross piece	2	pink	2	pink	2	pink	2	pink
tie-in	1	green	←———		1	green	←———	
cross piece	3	pink	3	pink	3	pink	3	pink
tie-in	1	green	1	green	←———		———→	
cross piece	4	pink	4	pink	4	pink	4	pink
tie-in	1	green	←———		1	green	←———	
cross piece	4	pink	4	pink	4	pink	4	pink
tie-in	1	green	1	green	←———		———→	
cross piece	3	pink	3	pink	3	pink	3	pink
tie-in	1	green	←———		1	green	←———	
cross piece	2	pink	2	pink	2	pink	2	pink
spoke lining	5	pink	5	pink	←———		———→	

How do you know when you have enough spokes and its time to lace-up? I count the bottom spokes, and when I have the number called for in the pattern, the next up-column is the lace-up column. You can also count top spokes and when you have the pattern max, the next up-column is lace-up.

(2) The basket is finished in the usual way: take off the stop bead and thread a second needle onto the tail thread. It might be a little difficult to take up all of the slack in the lace-up column so spend a little time tightening things up. When you are satisfied with the tension, pass the tail needle down through the first five green beads on the eighteenth down column and tie off. Using the working needle, go through the first bead on the first down column and tie off once. Inspect your work.

(3) Hold the piece in both hands with the lining upward and with your thumbs, invert the lining and push it down into the exterior portion of the net so that the two sets of

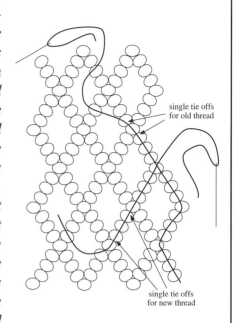

single tie offs
for old thread

single tie offs
for new thread

Two or three times during the construction of baskets and bottle covers you will run out of working thread and need to work in another 72 inch length. It is best to switch threads while working on the lining since it won't show as much. Try to make the switch in the middle of the lining around the longest cross pieces. On either a down- or up-column, go through a tie-in bead and continue up the cross-piece to the next tie-in bead (see digram). Tie off once, go through the tie-in bead and tie off again. Do not cut your thread yet. Pick up the second needle and thread it with a 72 inch length of thread. With the new needle, go through the beads of the cross piece two cross pieces below and to the left of where you left off (see diagram). Pull most of the new thread through the beads, leaving about 3 inches. With your fingers tie a single knot, but don't clip it yet. With the new needle, tie off once more before working your way through the tie-in bead where you left off. Leave the needle and thread in place until you are sure your pattern is correct and you don't need to undo any of it. When you are sure you don't need to take any of it out, glue both the old and new threads and cut close when dry or burn down carefully.

spokes meet. Line up the exterior and lining spokes properly by tracing the diamond shaped spaces to where they meet at the juncture of the exterior portion of the net and the lining. Remember that an exterior spoke will fall between two lining spokes and vice versa. Put a long sewing pin through both layers to hold the position of the spokes.

④ Using the working needle, anchor the exterior spoke row to the lining spoke row in the same manner as described in Chapter 3. Anchoring baskets is more difficult than simple flat nets because of the bulk of the basket and the number of spokes. After some practice, I found it easier to work this process while viewing it mostly from the bottom outside. In other words it will be easier to keep track of where you are and where the needle needs to go if you navigate from a single vantage point. Tie off both the working and tail threads and glue or burn down. Fini!

——Bottle Cover——

Bottle covers are very similar to large and slightly misshapen ball nets. Also they often need a small modification around one set of spokes since the spokes that surround the bottle's neck may need to be more widely spaced than the spokes under the bottom of the bottle. Covering bottles is a lot of fun and spherical nets offer a flexible method of constructing covers that can be adapted to any size and shape of bottle or other solid object.

The bottle that will be used in this exercise is small and quite common: a "Liquid Paper Correction Fluid" or "White-Out" bottle. Granted it is not very elegant but will serve to illustrate the principal features of bottle covers. In Chapter 9 patterns for two larger bottle covers are presented in detail along with one for a glass Christmas tree ornament. The bottles and glass ornament are available commercially. See Appendix A: Sources of Supplies for some sources for bottles and ornaments.

It should be noted that the "top" of the net will actually be situated at the bottom of the bottle and the "bottom" of the net will be at the top of the bottle surrounding the bottle neck. The reason for this is that the tie-offs will then be under the bottle where they are easier to execute without the bottle neck getting in the way. Also the knots are out of sight.

Covered "White-Out" bottle, shown approximately actual size. Individual beads are not shown.

Two colors of beads will be used: a dark color for the spokes and cross-pieces and a light color for the tie-ins. This will make the tie-ins easier to find and it is a rather pleasing pattern to boot. For the white-out bottle cover you will need:

Thread: 2 lengths of size D Nymo or upholstery thread, each about 60 inches long (cut as needed)

Needle: two thin but sturdy needles (John James #12 sharps)

Beads: two colors of size 10/0 and/or 11/0 beads with good sized holes. The instructions will refer to green and pink beads.

Other: one 3/4 oz. white-out bottle with label removed. [Old labels can be soaked off in hot, soapy water. With newer labels, WD-40 will help dissolve the label glue.]

① Thread your needle and put on a stop bead leaving about 6 inches in your tail thread. Use the following table for the sequence of beads for the down- and up-columns. At the bottom of each down-column put on an <u>extra green bead</u> before putting on the spoke beads in the next up-column. This will let the spokes at the bottom of the net, which go around the neck of the bottle, have a larger interior diameter. Be sure on the next down-column not to go through this extra bead. Check the fit of the bottle as you get close to the end. Before you do the lace-up column, insert the bottle so that the neck sticks out between the bottom spokes where the extra beads are.

Section	1st Dn		1-15th Up		2-16th Dn		16th Up	
spoke top	3	green	<———		3	green	<———	
cross piece	2	green	2	green	2	green	2	green
tie-in	1	pink	1	pink	<———		———>	
cross piece	3	green	3	green	3	green	3	green
tie-in	1	pink	<———		1	pink	<———	
cross piece	3	green	3	green	3	green	3	green
tie-in	1	pink	1	pink	<———		———>	
cross piece	3	green	3	green	3	green	3	green
tie-in	1	pink	<———		1	pink	<———	
cross piece	3	green	3	green	3	green	3	green
tie-in	1	pink	1	pink	<———		———>	
cross piece	3	green	3	green	3	green	3	green
tie-in	1	pink	<———		1	pink	<———	
cross piece	3	green	3	green	3	green	3	green
tie-in	1	pink	1	pink	<———		———>	
cross piece	3	green	3	green	3	green	3	green
tie-in	1	pink	<———		1	pink	<———	
cross piece	3	green	3	green	3	green	3	green
tie-in	1	pink	1	pink	<———		———>	
cross piece	3	green	3	green	3	green	3	green
tie-in	1	pink	<———		1	pink	<———	
cross piece	2	green	2	green	2	green	2	green
spoke bottom	3	green	3	green	<———		———>	
extra bead	**1**	**green**			**1**	**green**		

② Take off the stop bead, thread a second needle onto the tail thread. Since the net is stretched over a solid object, it may be difficult to get the slack out of the net prior to tying off. The tie off sequence is the same as for the basket: go through the three spoke beads of the 16th column with the tail thread, tie off once, go through two beads in the next cross piece and tie off a second time. In a similar manner go through the three spoke beads of the first column with the working thread, tie off once, go through two beads in the next cross piece and tie off a second time. Glue each thread t the knot and cut close when dry or burn down carefully.

When designing bead covers for bottles and large beads, the first thing one must do is decide on the number of cross-pieces and the number of beads in each cross-piece. The number of cross-pieces must be an odd number (1, 3,17, etc.) and the number of beads in a particular cross-piece will depend on the relative diameter of the bottle at the place where the cross-piece will lie. For the white-out bottle, the cross-pieces all had three beads in them (except at the top and bottom) because the bottle has a uniform diameter from top to bottom.

——**A Word on Net**——
Stretchability

You don't have to decide on the number of spokes (which equals the number of up- or down-columns), however, until you are nearly finished with the cover. You can always add or subtract one or two spokes, depending on how the cover actually fits the bottle or bead. The idea is that <u>these nets are stretchy</u>. You can make up for a too-short column length by adding more columns. On the other hand, if your column is too long, you can shorten it by subtracting a spoke and making the net stretch wider. Thus, the number of spokes can compensate for the length of the column.

In Chapter 7 two ball nets are presented that cover 16 mm beads. One ball net has 19 beads per column and six spokes, while the other has 17 beads per column and eight spokes. The size of net you make will depend a lot on the size of beads you use. If you tend to use tall 2-cut beads, or 9/0 or 10/0 beads, your nets may be "generous" for the interior bead specified in the pattern. To compensate, simply make the net with one or two fewer spokes. If you occasionally throw in a 15/0 bead or two, you may need to add a column or two to compensate. Because you may need to make fewer or more columns than specified in a pattern, start checking the size of your net against the size of the bottle or interior bead a few spokes short of the number specified in the pattern. Then check again after every down-column to see if the next up-column should be the last or lace-up column.

Although most of the bead and bottle cover patterns in this book specify an even number of spokes (6, 8, 18, etc.), there is no reason that they cannot have odd numbers of spokes. When I make a necklace that has several covered beads, I vary the number of beads per column, number of spokes and placement of colors within the pattern. This makes for a more interesting piece since the covered beads are not all the same.

Note: Bead and bottle covers may have any number of spokes, even or odd. This also goes for baskets. Flat nets, however, that are made into off-center stud earrings or tie-tack pins should have an even number of spokes. The reason is that both the stud part of the wire and the bottom loop need to hide behind a front spoke. If the flat net has an odd number of spokes, one or the other would show from the front.

7 Projects with Ball Nets

This chapter contains five projects arranged in three sections. The first section has patterns for covering 16 and 20 mm beads, in addition to the 12 mm interior bead used in Chapter 3. The second section uses 12 mm covered beads in a pair of simple earrings and as component beads in a necklace that is chained together. The third section contains the pattern for a pair of earrings made from a drop net hanging from a flat net.

Two different ball net patterns will be given which cover 16 mm interior beads. The first has 19 beads per column and 6 spokes. The second has 17 beads per column and 8 spokes. This is a good illustration of the flexibility of bead net covers which will come in handy when you design your own. It is sometimes hard to judge how many beads to put in a column and you cannot add any after you have started. You can, however, add down- and up-columns if your net is too small. This may happen if your beads are smaller than the ones used here. If your beads are larger you may not need as many down- and up-columns as specified. Check the size of the net against the interior item (bead or bottle) as you approach the final columns. This is especially important for larger items such as bottles.

Thread: 42 inches of size D Nymo or upholstery thread.

Needle: two thin but sturdy needles (John James #12 sharps)

Beads: six colors of size 10/0 and/or 11/0 beads with good sized holes. Choose three beads of a primary color, such as light, medium and dark blue, and three of a complementary secondary color, such as light, medium and dark pink. The three primary colors will be designated a, b, and c. The three secondary colors will be designated x, y and z.

Other: one 16 mm bead of any material

Thread your needle and put on a stop bead, leaving a 6 inch tail thread. Using either bead chart below, make a ball net in the same manner as illustrated in Chapter 2. Be sure to insert the 16 mm interior bead prior to finishing the lace-up column (6th or 8th). Then tie off as usual.

16 mm Covered Beads

A 16 mm bead covered with a ball net made with 6 spokes and 19 beads per spoke. Above: actual size. Below: enlarged to show details.

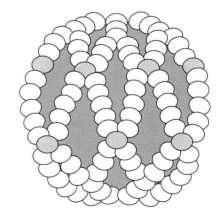

6 Spoke Net

Section	1st Dn	1-5th Up	2-6th Dn	6th Up
spoke top	3 abc	<———	3 abc	<———
cross piece	3 ccb	3 bcc	3 ccb	3 bcc
tie-in	1 a	1 a	<———	———>
bridge span	5 xyzyx	5 xyzyx	5 xyzyx	5 xyzyx
tie-in	1 a	<———	1 a	<———
cross piece	3 bcc	3 ccb	3 bcc	3 ccb
spoke bottom	3 cba	3 abc	<———	———>

8 Spoke Net

Section	1st Dn	1-7th Up	2-8th Dn	8th Up
spoke top	3 abc	<———	3 abc	<———
cross piece	2 ba	2 ab	2 ba	2 ab
tie-in	1 x	1 x	<———	———>
bridge span	5 yzzzy	5 yzzzy	5 yzzzy	5 yzzzy
tie-in	1 x	<———	1 x	<———
cross piece	2 ab	2 ba	2 ab	2 ba
spoke bottom	3 cba	3 abc	<———	———>

—20 mm Covered—
Beads

A 20 mm bead covered with a ball net made with 10 spokes and 21 beads per column. Above: actual size. Below: enlarged to show details.

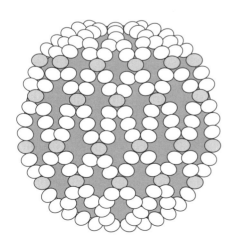

The 20 mm bead cover has 21 beads per column and 10 spokes. The short cross-piece and bridge-span sections make for a denser bead cover. For one 20mm bead cover you will need:

Thread: 48 inches of size D Nymo or upholstery thread.

Needle: two thin but sturdy needles (John James #12 sharps)

Beads: six colors of size 10/0 and/or 11/0 beads with good sized holes. Choose three beads of a primary color (designated a, b, and c) and three of a complementary secondary color (x, y and z).

Other: one 20 mm bead of any material

Thread your needle and put on a stop bead, leaving a 6 inch tail thread. Follow the bead chart. Insert the 20 mm interior bead prior to finishing the lace-up column. Then tie off as usual.

Section	1st Dn	1-9th Up	2-10th Dn	10th Up
spoke top	3 abc	<———	3 abc	<———
cross piece	2 xy	2 yx	2 xy	2 yx
tie-in	1 z	1 z	<———	———>
cross piece	2 yx	2 xy	2 yx	2 xy
tie-in	1 a	<———	1 a	<———
bridge span	3 bcb	3 bcb	3 bcb	3 bcb
tie-in	1 a	1 a	<———	———>
cross piece	2 xy	2 yx	2 xy	2 yx
tie-in	1 z	<———	1 z	<———
cross piece	2 yx	2 xy	2 yx	2 xy
spoke bottom	3 cba	3 abc	<———	———>

12 mm Covered Bead Earrings

Thread: two lengths of 24 inches of D Nymo or upholstery thread.

Needle: two thin but sturdy needles (John James #12 sharps)

Beads: six colors of size 10/0 and/or 11/0 beads with good sized holes. Choose three beads of a primary color and three of a complementary secondary color. The three primary colors will be designated a, b, and c. The three secondary colors will be designated x, y and z.

Other: Two 12 mm beads of any material. Four each of 2 mm and 3 mm gold colored metal beads and two 6 mm glass beads of a complementary color. Also two 2-3 inch gold head pins and ear hooks. Silver beads, head pins and ear hooks may be used if preferred.

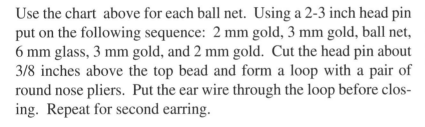

Section	1st Dn		1-7th Up		2-8th Dn		8th Up	
spoke top	3	ab	<———		3	ab	<———	
cross piece	2	ca	2	ac	2	ca	2	ac
tie-in	1	x	1	x	<———		———>	
bridge span	3	yzy	3	yzy	3	yzy	3	yzy
tie-in	1	x	<———		1	x	<———	
cross piece	2	ac	2	ca	2	ac	2	ca
spoke bottom	2	ba	2	ab	<———		———>	

Use the chart above for each ball net. Using a 2-3 inch head pin put on the following sequence: 2 mm gold, 3 mm gold, ball net, 6 mm glass, 3 mm gold, and 2 mm gold. Cut the head pin about 3/8 inches above the top bead and form a loop with a pair of round nose pliers. Put the ear wire through the loop before closing. Repeat for second earring.

A pair of earrings made with covered 12 mm beads. Shown actual size. A 12 mm covered bead is approximately 16 mm in diameter.

12 mm Covered Bead Necklace

This necklace consists of 15 sections and is about 30 inches long. Each section consists of a ball net and an 8 mm bead along with some 5 mm glass beads and 2 and 3 mm gold colored metal beads. Shorter and longer necklaces can be made by subtracting or adding sections, respectively. For each section you will need:

Thread: 24 inches of D Nymo or upholstery thread.

Needle: two thin but sturdy needles (John James #12 sharps)

Beads: six colors of size 10/0 and/or 11/0 beads with good sized holes. Choose three beads of a primary color and three of a complementary secondary color. The three primary colors will be designated a, b, and c. The three secondary colors will be designated x, y and z.

Two sections of a chain link necklace made with 12 mm covered beads. Shown actual size. A 12 mm covered bead is about 16 mm in diameter.

Other: one 12 mm bead of any material. Four 2 mm gold colored metal beads, one 8 mm and two 5 or 6 mm glass beads of a complementary color. You will also need about 3 inches of 20 gauge gold colored wire. If possible use a single length of wire for all sections and cut only as needed.

For each section construct a 12 mm covered bead using the same bead chart as for the earrings above. Take the long section of 20 gauge wire in your left hand. Put on a 2 mm gold bead, a 5 or 6 mm glass bead, a 12 mm covered bead, a 5 or 6 mm glass bead and a 2 mm gold bead. Make a loop in the end of the wire with a pair of round-nosed pliers. Turn the wire over and push the beads to the loop. Cut the wire 3/8 inches from the first 2 mm gold bead and form into a loop. For the next link in the chain put a 2 mm gold, 8 mm colored glass, and 2 mm gold bead on the wire. Form a loop, turn over, cut at 3/8 inch and form the second loop. Before closing this loop completely, hook it through one end of the link with the ball net. Close the loop.

Continue for as many sections as you want. It is probably easier to make all the covered beads and then do the chaining. Each section is about 2 inches so 15 sections will make a necklace which is 30 inches long. If you want a choker, use seven covered bead sections, add an extra 8 mm glass bead link to the back and a clasp. This will give you a 15 inch choker. Nine sections will make an 18 inch choker.

—Earrings of a Drop— Net and Flat Net

This earring consists of a drop net hanging from a flat net which has an off-center ear wire. The drop net is a type of ball net and uses a 12 mm round bead as one of the interior beads. The flat net is the smallest described in this book. The loop in the wire at the top of the drop net attaches to the loop made by the bottom of the ear wire on the flat net. The flat net has no cross-pieces or tie-ins, just top and bottom spoke rows and a single bead as a bridge-span. For each drop net you will need:

Thread: 30 inches of D Nymo or upholstery thread.

Needle: two thin but sturdy needles (John James #12 sharps)

Beads: Five colors of size 10/0 or 11/0 seed beads. See the Choose three beads of a primary color and two of a complementary secondary color. The three primary colors will be designated a, b, and c. The secondary colors will be designated x and y.

Other: One 12 mm interior bead plus a 5 mm bead and others which together make a column about 1.125 inches long. Two 2 mm gold colored metal beads and two 4 mm glass or crystal beads of a complementary color. A 2-3 inch head pin.

Section	1st Dn		1-5th Up		2-6th Dn		6th Up	
spoke top	3	abc	<———		3	abc	<———	
cross piece	1	b	1	b	1	b	1	b
tie-in	1	a	1	a	<———		———>	
cross piece	3	xyx	3	xyx	3	xyx	3	xyx
tie-in	1	a	<———		1	a	<———	
bridge span	3	bcb	3	bcb	3	bcb	3	bcb
tie-in	1	a	1	a	<———		———>	
cross piece	3	xyx	3	xyx	3	xyx	3	xyx
tie-in	1	a	<———		1	a	<———	
cross piece	3	bcb	3	bcb	3	bcb	3	bcb
spoke bottom	5	axyxa	5	axyxa	<———		———>	

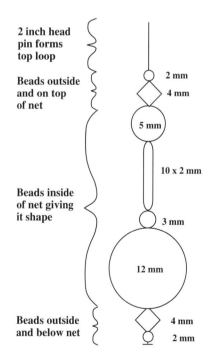

Pair of drop net earrings shown actual size (2.5 inches long).

Prior to putting on the final or lace-up column, insert the 12 mm bead. Finish with the lace-up column. **Before tying off**, take a head pin, and put on a 2 mm gold and 4 mm glass or crystal bead. Stick the head pin through the hole formed by the bottom spoke beads and through the 12 mm interior bead. Put on additional beads and then a 5 mm glass or metal bead. You may need to loosen the thread on the last up-column a little. The length of the column of beads on the head pin should be just short of the length of the drop net. Make sure the head pin wire sticks out the top of the net. When all of the beads have been put onto the head pin, put an ear nut on it so it won't slip out. Pull the thread tight so that the top spoke rows close over the top of the top 5 mm bead on the head pin. Tie off as for a ball net. Take the ear nut off the head pin (carefully - don't let i slip out) and put on a 4 mm glass or crystal bead and a 2 mm gold bead. With a pair of wire cutters, cut the head pin to 3/8 inch and make a loop with a pair of round-nosed pliers.

For each flat net you will need:

Thread: 20 inches of D Nymo or upholstery thread.

Needle: two thin but sturdy needles (John James #12 sharps)

Beads: Four colors of size 10/0 or 11/0 seed beads. Choose two beads of the primary color and two of the complementary secondary color. The two primary colors will be designated a and b. The secondary colors will be designated x and y.

2 inch head pin forms top loop

Beads outside and on top of net

2 mm
4 mm
5 mm
10 x 2 mm

Beads inside of net giving it shape

3 mm
12 mm

Beads outside and below net

4 mm
2 mm

The entire column of beads used with the drop net. Net fits over the 5 and 12 mm beads and those in between. The 4 and 2 mm beads are outside the drop net.

Other: One 6 mm center bead. A 23 mm (7/8 inches) length of 20 gauge, half-hard, gold-filled wire. Smooth the ends of the wire by rubbing them on a piece of 200-400 grit carbide sandpaper.

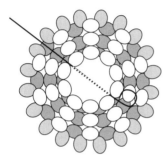

A 23 mm length of 20 gauge half-hard gold-filled wire with smoothed ends. One end has been formed into a loop using round-nosed pliers.

To make the drop net use the following chart. If you tend to have tight tension in your nets, ease up a little on this one. See the discussion of tension in Chapter 3.

Section	1st Dn		1-5th Up		2-6th Dn		6th Up	
spoke top	3	abx	<———		3	abx	<———	
bridge span	1	y	1	y	1	y	1	y
spoke bottom	3	xba	3	abx	<———		———>	

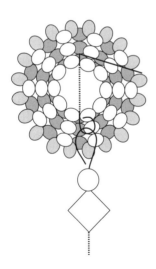

After inserting 6 mm center bead into the net and pushing it flat, insert the ear wire between two spokes, through the 6 mm bead, and out between two spokes on the opposite side. Then anchor the net.

(You might want to review the basics of constructing a flat net earring with an off-center stud in Chapter 4.) After finishing the lace-up column, take off the stop bead and put the second on the tail thread. Using the tail needle, go down through the top three beads of the 10th down column and tie off once. Using the working needle, go through the first bead of the first column and tie off once. Take the 23 mm length of 20 gauge wire and make a loop at one end with a pair of round-nosed pliers. Flatten the net and insert the 6 mm bead through the hole formed by the top row of spokes. Insert the straight end of the 20 gauge wire between two top spokes, through the 6 mm bead and out between two spokes exactly opposite from where it went in. Count to make sure there are 5 spokes on either side of the ear wire. Anchor the flat net as described in Chapter 3 and tie off. Bend the 20 gauge ear wire at a right angle (90°) to the plane of the flat net at a point just above the 6 mm center bead.

To attach the drop net to the flat net, open the loop on the drop net a little and hook it through the bottom loop on the flat net. Close both loops securely. Use a comfort clutch. A drop net can also be hung off a regular stud, ear hook or ear clip.

Bend the ear wire 90 degrees just above where it comes out of the 6 mm center bead. Open the loop on the drop net a little and hook it through the loop on the bottom of the flat net. Use a comfort clutch to hold the earring in place.

8 Flat Net Projects

This chapter contains eight projects using flat nets. The first two projects are central stud earrings, one a plain disk and the second a smaller flat net with fringe. The second set of projects consists of 4 flat net earrings with off center studs with different numbers of spokes and cross-pieces. The third set consists of two projects for pins, one with a stick pin as the pinning device and the second which uses a tie-tack closure or "keeper".

A convention for naming different configurations of spherical nets is needed. The one that will be used here specifies the number of spokes and the number of cross-pieces and bridge-spans. For example, the pin in this Chapter with a stick pin closure has 10 spokes, 3 cross-pieces per side and one bridge-span. Its name is "10s7c pin". A net that is used as an earring or pin with dangles, has the number of dangles appended. Thus, " 8s3c9d" is the second project in this chapter, the details of which were introduced in Chapter 5. This convention does not entirely specify a spherical net since no mention is made of the number of beads in each cross-piece, bridge-span or spoke. It does, however, give us a starting point from which to elaborate.

Naming Spherical Nets

This is the largest flat net earring style for the central stud and one of my favorites. It can also be made with an ear clip for non-pierced ears (see "Clip Earrings" in this Chapter). For each earring you will need:

Thread: 42 inches of size D Nymo or upholstery thread.

Needle: two thin but sturdy needles (John James #12 sharps)

Beads: six colors of size 10/0 and/or 11/0 beads with good sized holes. Choose three beads of a primary color and three of a complementary secondary color. The three primary colors will be designated a, b, and c. The three secondary colors will be designated x, y and z.

Other: One 4 to 5 mm center bead, a 4 mm soldered ring and a 4 mm cup or 6 mm flat earring stud.

Thread your needle and put on a stop bead, leaving a 6 inch tail thread. Use the chart below, making sure to incorporate the soldered ring as discussed in Chapter 4. Remember that you include it in the loop of beads made by the bottom spokes of the

8s5c Flat Net Earrings with Central Studs

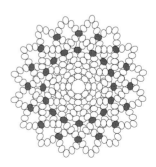

The 8s5c flat net earring is made with a central stud, shown actual size (about 1.5 inches in diameter).

first down- and up-columns. Then after you put on the second down-column, pull the soldered ring to the thread between the two spokes and rotate it 90° (one quarter of a circle) clockwise so it lies in the same plane as your beads. Then pass your needle down through the ring before starting on the up-column. Do this on all subsequent down-columns including the last one.

Section	1st Dn		1-7th Up		2-8th Dn		8th Up	
spoke top	3	abc	<———		3	abc	<———	
cross piece	2	ba	2	ab	2	ba	2	ab
tie-in	1	x	1	x	<———		———>	
cross piece	3	yzy	3	yzy	3	yzy	3	yzy
tie-in	1	x	<———		1	x	<———	
bridge span	5	abcba	5	abcba	5	abcba	5	abcba
tie-in	1	x	1	x	<———		———>	
cross piece	3	yzy	3	yzy	3	yzy	3	yzy
tie-in	1	x	<———		1	x	<———	
cross piece	2	ab	2	ba	2	ab	2	ba
spoke bottom	3	cba	3	abc	<———		———>	

s o l d e r e d   j u m p   r i n g

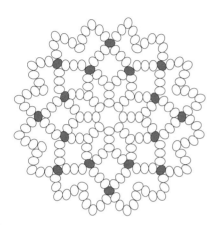

The 8s5c flat net earring shown with top of net and bridge-span only. Shown larger than actual size.

Finish the earring in the same manner that you did in Chapter 4. Recall that you take off the stop bead and thread a needle onto the tail thread. Pass the tail thread down through the top three beads of the 8th down-column and tie off once. Then with the working needle, put on the 4-5 mm center bead and go through the first bead in the 4th column and tie off. Insert the 4 mm cup or 6 mm flat stud, sticking the stem out the back through the soldered ring so that the cup or pad rests behind the 4-5 mm center bead. Anchor the flat net as described in Chapter 3 and tie off.

—8s3c9d Flat Net— Earrings with Central Studs

The bead arrangement for this earring is exactly the same as that for the earring in the first half of Chapter 5 where the attachment of fringes was introduced. The purpose for it reappearing here is to discuss color combinations and to condense the pattern into a single word chart. These earrings can also be made with ear clips for non-pierced ears (see "Clip Earrings" in this Chapter). For the flat net base of each earring you will need:

Thread: 24 inches of size D Nymo or upholstery thread..

Needle: two thin but sturdy needles (John James #12 sharps)

Beads: six colors of size 10/0 and/or 11/0 beads with good sized holes. Choose three beads of a primary color and three of a complementary secondary color. The three primary colors will be designated a, b, and c. The three secondary colors will be designated x, y and z.

Other: One 4 to 5 mm center bead, a 4 mm soldered ring and a 4 mm cup or 6 mm flat earring stud.

Thread your needle and put on a stop bead, leaving a 6 inch tail thread. Use the chart below, making sure to incorporate the soldered ring as discussed in Chapter 4 or above for the 8s5c flat net earring.

Section	1st Dn		1-7th Up		2-7th Dn		8th Up	
spoke top	3	abc	<———		3	abc	<———	
cross piece	2	xy	2	yx	2	xy	2	yx
tie-in	1	z	1	z	<———		———>	
bridge span	2	aa	2	aa	2	aa	2	aa
tie-in	1	z	<———		1	z	<———	
cross piece	2	yx	2	xy	2	yx	2	xy
spoke bottom	3	cba	3	abc	<———		———>	

s o l d e r e d   j u m p   r i n g

For the fringe of each earring you will need:

Thread: 72 inches of size C or D Nymo thread

Needle: 1 size13 long bead needle and a shorter #12.

Beads: Same six colors of size 10/0 or 11/0 seed beads that you used for the base. The three primary colors will be designated a, b, and c. The three secondary colors will be designated x, y and z.

Other: Nine 4-6 mm beads for the fringe bottom in the primary color, nine 6/0 to 8/0 or "pony" beads in the secondary color and nine 20 mm bugles in the primary color.

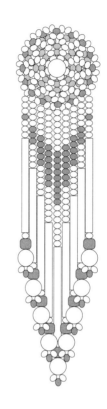

The 8s3c9d flat net earring with nine dangles, shown actual size.

Thread your needle. Use the instructions in Chapter 5 for making the fringe according to the color chart below. This is essentially the same as the chart used in Chapter 5 except that each color is expanded into its three component beads. The blank spaces in the "xyzyx" section simply mean the y and z beads are not included in the outer dangles. The spaces should not be interpreted to mean that any thread is left bare.

Dangle#	9	8	7	6	5	4	3	2	1
Beads	f	c	b	c	f	c	b	c	f
a	1	2	2	3	3	3	2	2	1
b	1	1	2	2	3	2	2	1	1
c	1	1	1	1	1	1	1	1	1
x	1	1	1	2	2	2	1	1	1
y		1	1	1	1	1	1	1	
z			1	1	3	1	1		
y			1	1	1	1	1		
x		1	1	2	2	2	1	1	
c	1	1	1	1	1	1	1	1	1
b	1	1	2	2	3	2	2	1	1
a	1	2	2	3	3	3	2	2	1
bugle	1	1	1	1	1	1	1	1	1
y	1	1	1	1	1	1	1	1	1
pony	1	1	1	1	1	1	1	1	1
4-5mm	1	1	1	1	1	1	1	1	1
triplet	1	1	1	1	1	1	1	1	1

Many variations of this fringe pattern are possible. For the seed bead sections above the bugle beads, the rule of thumb is to add 4 beads to each dangle as you work your way from the outer edge to the center. To get a gradual increase in the colors, one bead is added to each of the top and bottom "abc" sections and two beads are added to the middle "xyzyx" section. This gives a fringe with the center dangle about an inch or 25 mm longer than the edge dangles.

To make a longer fringe you could use 25 or 30 mm bugles or start off with more beads in the "abc" or "xyzyx" sections. Instead of a single bugle you could also use combinations of shorter bugles. A combination of a #2 and a #5 bugle with a single contrasting seed bead in between is nice, as are 3 #2s separated by single seeds. The latter pattern was used on the dangle earrings on the front cover.

—— Clip Earrings ——

The best type of ear clip for attaching to a flat net is one with a 20 mm pad, perforated with 21 holes in the pattern shown above.

You can make either style of central stud earrings into clip earrings. In general, you do not include a soldered ring as you construct the flat net. Use a slightly longer thread and leave a 10 inch tail. When you have finished the flat net, anchor it as in Chapter 3 and attach an ear clip with a perforated 15 mm diameter pad.

After finishing the lace-up column on either the 8s5c or 8s3c9d flat net, take off the stop bead and thread a needle onto the tail thread. Pass the tail thread down through the first bead of the 8th down column and tie off once. Then with the working needle, put on the 4-5 mm center bead and go through the first bead in the 4th column and tie off. Anchor the flat net as described in Chapter 3. After you have anchored the flat net all the way around the center bead, bring the thread to the back of the net and go through the second bead of either adjacent spoke and tie off once. Stick the tail needle down through the net and go through the second bead only of the spoke directly opposite from where the working thread is tied off and tie off the tail thread once.

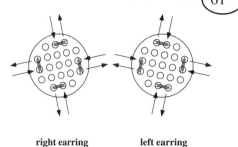

right earring   left earring

Perforated 15 mm disks showing opposite orientations for right and left earrings.

Place the ear clip to the back of the net and secure it by looping the working thread between the second and third bead of its spoke and two edge holes of the base of the ear clip. Make three loops with the thread and come out between the flat net and the ear clip base. Then do the same looping between the spoke two spokes over (in either direction) and the holes in the ear clip base right over them. Tie off and glue the knot. Burning it down might be tricky in this instance. Do the same for the other two corners using the tail thread.

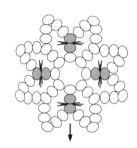

The back of the flat net showing only the spokes and first cross-piece sections. Horizontal and vertical lines indicate the placement of the thread for attachment of the ear clip base.

A word of caution: be gentle with the threads when securing an ear clip. The holes in the ear clip base can be sharp and may wear through your threads. I have found, however, that once attached, the ear clip stays on for a long time.

Alignment of the clip is not very important with the 8s5c flat nets since there is no inherent up-down orientation. There is, however, with the 8s3c9d flat net since it has a fringe which must go down. Using the above technique it is not possible to have the ear clip exactly in line with the dangles. The "angle of error", however, is less than 12° or 1/32nd of a circle. This is tolerable. However, since each earring should be a mirror image of the other one, put the "angle of error" on opposite sides of the center dangle. On both earrings use the back spoke that is directly above the center dangle for securing to the holes nearest the ear clip base. See diagrams. On one earring use the left and center holes on the ear base and on the other earring use the right and center holes.

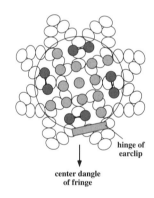

hinge of earclip

center dangle of fringe

Placement of the earclip on the back of the flat net for the right earring. The base of the ear clip is a little to the right of the center dangle on the 8s3c9d earring.

This pair of earrings and the two that follow have pretty much the same pattern, except for size of center bead and number of spokes. In general, flat nets with off- center studs are more difficult to convert to clip earrings. The main reason for this is that since they are larger, the ear clip needs to be anchored off-center so that most of the weight of the earring is below the clip. In this position, however, the clip may show from the front. If you do attempt to attach an ear clip, attach the center bead using the working thread as for the 8s5c earring.

——10s5c Flat Net—— Earrings with Off-center Studs

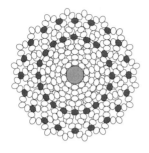

For each 10s5c flat net earring you will need:

Thread: 48 inches of size D Nymo or upholstery thread.

Needle: 2 thin but sturdy needles (John James #12 sharps)

Beads: Six colors of size 10/0 or 11/0 seed beads. Choose three beads of a primary color and three of a complementary secondary color. The three primary colors will be designated a, b, and c. The three secondary colors will be designated x, y and z.

Other: One 6 mm center bead and 35 mm of 20 gauge, half-hard, gold filled wire. 20 gauge, half-hard silver wire may also be used. Smooth both ends of the ear wire on a piece of fine grit carbide sandpaper.

The 10s5c earring with an off-center stud is shown above about actual size. Below, the top half of the flat net with the bridge-span row is shown.

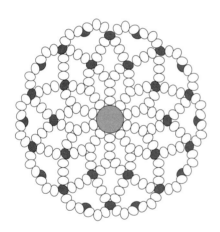

Thread your needle and put on a stop bead, leaving a 6 inch tail thread. Use the chart below. Finish in the same manner as for the off center stud earring described in Chapter 4. The steps are briefly repeated below.

Section	1st Dn		1-9th Up		2-10th Dn		10th Up	
spoke top	3	abc	<———		3	abc	<———	
cross piece	2	ba	2	ab	2	ba	2	ab
tie-in	1	x	1	x	<———		———>	
cross piece	3	yzy	3	yzy	3	yzy	3	yzy
tie-in	1	x	<———		1	x	<———	
bridge span	3	bcb	3	bcb	3	bcb	3	bcb
tie-in	1	x	1	x	<———		———>	
cross piece	3	yzy	3	yzy	3	yzy	3	yzy
tie-in	1	x	<———		1	x	<———	
cross piece	2	ab	2	ba	2	ab	2	ba
spoke bottom	3	cba	3	abc	<———		———>	

After the lace-up column, take off the stop bead and thread the tail needle onto the tail thread. Put it down through the three beads of the 10th top spoke and tie off once. Using the working thread, go down through the first bead only of the first down-column and tie off once. Make a loop in one end of the 20 gauge, half-hard wire with a pair of round-nosed pliers. Insert the center bead into the interior of the flat net and squash it flat, trapping the center bead in the holes formed by the top and bottom spokes. Insert the wire between two top spokes, through the 6 mm bead and out between two top spokes on the opposite side of the flat net. Make sure there are five spokes on either side of the wire. Hold the flat net in your left hand, making sure the center bead and ear wire stay in place, while you anchor the flat net using the working thread. After you have worked the anchoring thread all the way around the center bead, go down through the second and third beads of the first down-column and tie off. Finish by gluing the last knots on both the tail and working threads and cutting when dry or cutting to a quarter inch (6 mm) first and burning down carefully. Note that the "top" of the spherical net becomes the "back" of the flat net earring when you attach off-center studs.

12s5c Flat Net Earrings with Off-center Studs

This pair of earrings takes a 7 mm center bead. These are rather rare in the world of beads but I have actually found some 7 mm Swarovsky faceted crystal and black onyx stone beads. The main difference between this and the 10s5c flat net is the number of spokes. The 7 mm center bead needs 12 spokes to fit around it comfortably. For each 12s5c flat net earring you will need:

Thread: 54 inches of size D Nymo or upholstery thread.

Needle: 2 thin but sturdy needles (John James #12 sharps)

Beads: Six colors of size 10/0 or 11/0 seed beads. Choose three beads of a primary color and three of a complementary secondary color. The three primary colors will be designated a, b, and c. The three secondary colors will be designated x, y and z.

Other: One 7 mm center bead and one 35 mm length of 20 gauge, half-hard, gold filled wire. 20 gauge, half-hard silver wire may also be used. Smooth both ends of the ear wire on a piece of fine grit carbide sandpaper.

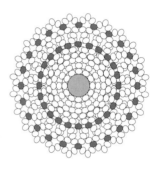

12s5c flat net earring with an off-center stud is shown above approximately actual size. Below is the top half of flat net with the bridge-span row.

Thread your needle and put on a stop bead, leaving a 6 inch tail thread. Use the chart below. The finish is the same as for the off center stud earring described in Chapter 4 or you can use the steps repeated above for the 10s5c flat net.

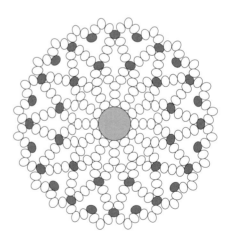

Section	1st Dn		1-10th Up		2-12th Dn		12th Up	
spoke top	3	abc	<———		3	abc	<———	
cross piece	2	ba	2	ab	2	ba	2	ab
tie-in	1	x	1	x	<———		———>	
cross piece	3	yzy	3	yzy	3	yzy	3	yzy
tie-in	1	x	<———		1	x	<———	
bridge span	3	bcb	3	bcb	3	bcb	3	bcb
tie-in	1	x	1	x	<———		———>	
cross piece	3	yzy	3	yzy	3	yzy	3	yzy
tie-in	1	x	<———		1	x	<———	
cross piece	2	ab	2	ba	2	ab	2	ba
spoke bottom	3	cba	3	abc	<———		———>	

14s5c Flat Net Earrings with Off-center Studs

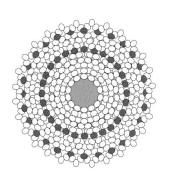

The 14s7c flat net can be finished as an off-center stud earring. Above is the full flat net and below is the top half of the net only. It is shown above approximately actual size while below it is larger to allow more detail.

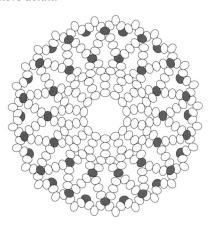

This pair of earrings takes an 8 mm center bead. An 8 mm center bead needs 14 spokes to fit around it comfortably. For each 14s5c flat net earring you will need:

Thread: 72 inches of D Nymo or upholstery thread

Needle: 2 thin but sturdy needles (John James #12 sharps)

Beads: Six colors of size 10/0 or 11/0 seed beads. Choose three beads of a primary color and three of a complementary secondary color. The three primary colors will be designated a, b, and c. The three secondary colors will be designated x, y and z.

Other: One 8 mm center bead and a 40 mm length of 20-gauge, half-hard, gold filled wire. 20-gauge, half-hard silver wire may also be used. Smooth both ends of the ear wire on a piece of fine grit carbide sandpaper.

Thread your needle and put on a stop bead, leaving a 6 inch tail thread. Use the chart below. The finish is the same as for the off center stud earring described in Chapter 4 or you can use the steps repeated above for the 10s5c flat net.

Section	1st Dn		1-13th Up		2-14th Dn		14th Up	
spoke top	3	abc	<————		3	abc	<————	
cross piece	2	ba	2	ab	2	ba	2	ab
tie-in	1	x	1	x	<————		————>	
cross piece	3	yzy	3	yzy	3	yzy	3	yzy
tie-in	1	x	<————		1	x	<————	
bridge span	3	bcb	3	bcb	3	bcb	3	bcb
tie-in	1	x	1	x	<————		————>	
cross piece	3	yzy	3	yzy	3	yzy	3	yzy
tie-in	1	x	<————		1	x	<————	
cross piece	2	ab	2	ba	2	ab	2	ba
spoke bottom	3	cba	3	abc	<————		————>	

10s7c Flat Net Earrings with Off-center Studs

This flat net takes a 6 mm center bead and has 10 spokes. With two more cross-pieces, the 10s7c flat net makes a very large earring which is surprisingly light. For each 10s7c flat net earring you will need:

Thread: 60 inches of size D Nymo or upholstery thread.

Needle: 2 thin but sturdy needles (John James #12 sharps)

Beads: Six colors of size 10/0 or 11/0 seed beads. Choose three beads of a primary color and three of a complementary secondary color. The three primary colors will be a, b, and c. The three secondary colors, x, y and z.

Other: One 6 mm center bead and 40 mm length of 20-gauge, half-hard, gold filled wire. 20-gauge, half-hard silver wire may also be used. Smooth both ends of the ear wire on a piece of fine grit carbide sand-paper.

Thread your needle and put on a stop bead, leaving a 6 inch tail thread. Use the chart below. The finish is the same as for the off-center stud earring described in Chapter 4 or you can use the steps repeated above for the 10s5c flat net.

Section	1st Dn		1-9th Up		2-10th Dn		10th Up	
spoke top	3	abc	< ———		3	abc	< ———	
cross piece	2	ba	2	ab	2	ba	2	ab
tie-in	1	x	1	x	< ———		——— >	
cross piece	3	yzy	3	yzy	3	yzy	3	yzy
tie-in	1	x	< ———		1	x	< ———	
cross piece	4	abcb	4	bcba	4	abcb	4	bcba
tie-in	1	a	1	a	< ———		——— >	
bridge span	5	xyzyx	5	xyzyx	5	xyzyx	5	xyzyx
tie-in	1	a	< ———		1	a	< ———	
cross piece	4	bcba	4	abcb	4	bcba	4	abcb
tie-in	1	x	1	x	< ———		——— >	
cross piece	3	yzy	3	yzy	3	yzy	3	yzy
tie-in	1	x	< ———		1	x	< ———	
cross piece	2	ab	2	ba	2	ab	2	ba
spoke bottom	3	cba	3	abc	< ———		——— >	

The 10s7c flat net can be finished as an off-center stud earring. Above is the full flat net and below is the top half of the net only. It is shown approximately actual size.

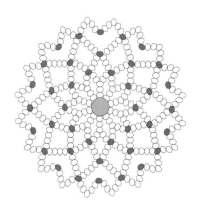

The two pins described in this chapter are each about 2 inches in diameter. They each have three pairs of cross pieces. The first pin has 10 spokes, takes a 6 mm center bead and uses a stick pin as a pinning device. The flat net for this pin is the same as that for the 10s7c pair of earrings. The second pin has 14 spokes, takes an 8 mm center bead and uses a tie-tack as a pinning device. For the 10s7c flat net pin you will need:

10s7c Flat Net Pin with Stick Pin Closure

Thread: 60 inches of size D Nymo or upholstery thread.

Needle: 2 thin but sturdy needles (John James #12 sharps)

Beads: Six colors of size 10/0 or 11/0 seed beads. Choose three beads of a primary color and three of a complementary secondary color. The three primary colors will be designated a, b, and c. The three secondary colors will be designated x, y and z.

Other: Two 6 mm beads, one for the center of the flat net and the other for the stick pin. A stiff 3 inch gold or silver colored head pin. If you cannot find a stiff head pin, you can use a 3 inch length of 20 gauge, half-hard,

The 10s7c flat net can also be finished as a pin which is fastened with a stick pin tipped with an ear stud comfort clutch. It is shown here approximately actual size.

gold-filled or silver wire. Sharpen one end of wire or head pin on fine grit carbide sandpaper.

Thread your needle and put on a stop bead, leaving a 6 inch tail thread. Use the chart below.

Section	1st Dn		1-9th Up		2-10th Dn		10th Up	
spoke top	3	abc	<———		3	abc	<———	
cross piece	2	ba	2	ab	2	ba	2	ab
tie-in	1	x	1	x	<———		———>	
cross piece	3	yzy	3	yzy	3	yzy	3	yzy
tie-in	1	x	<———		1	x	<———	
cross piece	4	abcb	4	bcba	4	abcb	4	bcba
tie-in	1	a	1	a	<———		———>	
bridge span	5	xyzyx	5	xyzyx	5	xyzyx	5	xyzyx
tie-in	1	a	<———		1	a	<———	
cross piece	4	bcba	4	abcb	4	bcba	4	abcb
tie-in	1	x	1	x	<———		———>	
cross piece	3	yzy	3	yzy	3	yzy	3	yzy
tie-in	1	x	<———		1	x	<———	
cross piece	2	ab	2	ba	2	ab	2	ba
spoke bottom	3	cba	3	abc	<———		———>	

Finish the pin in the same manner that you did the flat net in Chapter 3. Recall that you take off the stop bead and thread a tail needle onto the tail thread. Pass the tail thread down through the top three beads of the 10th down column and tie off once. Then with the working needle, put on the 6 mm center bead and go through the first bead in the 5th column and tie off. Anchor the flat net as described in Chapter 3. After you have worked the anchoring thread all the way around the center bead, bring it to the back of the pin. Go down through the second and third bead of an adjacent spoke and tie off. Finish by gluing the last knots on both the tail and working threads and cutting when dry or cutting to a quarter inch (6 mm) and burning down carefully.

If you use a 3 inch piece of wire for the stick pin, glue a 2 mm gold or silver colored (matching) bead onto the blunt end using epoxy glue. Or you can mash a crimp bead onto the end with a crimping tool. Put a 6 mm bead onto the head pin or wire and a seed bead if desired and if you can find one that has a large enough hole. To hold these beads in place, use a 2 mm metal bead and epoxy it in place or use another crimp bead. To use the stick pin, place the flat net where you want it and stick the pin through an outer space, under the material, and out an outer space on the opposite side of the flat net. Secure the pin with an ear nut, preferably a comfort clutch without the plastic rim.

14s7c Flat Net Pin with Tie-tack Closure

This pin has 14 spokes, takes an 8 mm center bead and uses a tie-tack as a pinning device. You don't actually use a tie-tack stud, but instead use an inch length of 18 gauge, gold or silver colored wire. The clutch, however, is a commercially purchased tie-tack clutch. For the 14s7c flat net pin you will need:

Thread: 72 inches of size D Nymo or upholstery thread.

Needle: 2 thin but sturdy needles (John James #12 sharps)

Beads: Six colors of size 10/0 or 11/0 seed beads. Choose three beads of a primary color and three of a complementary secondary color. The three primary colors will be designated a, b, and c. The three secondary colors will be designated x, y and z.

Other: One 8 mm center bead. 25 mm (1 inch) length of 18 gauge brass or nickle wire. Sharpen one end of the wire on fine grit carbide sandpaper and polish it with a rouge cloth.

The 14s7c flat net can be used as a pin with a tie-tack style fastener. This illustration is approximately actual size.

Thread your needle and put on a stop bead, leaving a 6 inch tail thread. Use the chart below. Note that this is the same chart as for the 10 spoke pin except that there are 14 spokes and only 3 beads in the bridge span.

Section	1st Dn		1-13th Up		2-14th Dn		14th Up	
spoke top	3	abc	<———		3	abc	<———	
cross piece	2	ba	2	ab	2	ba	2	ab
tie-in	1	x	1	x	<———		———>	
cross piece	3	yzy	3	yzy	3	yzy	3	yzy
tie-in	1	x	<———		1	x	<———	
cross piece	4	abcb	4	bcba	4	abcb	4	bcba
tie-in	1	a	1	a	<———		———>	
bridge span	3	yzy	3	yzy	3	yzy	3	yzy
tie-in	1	a	<———		1	a	<———	
cross piece	4	bcba	4	abcb	4	bcba	4	abcb
tie-in	1	x	1	x	<———		———>	
cross piece	3	yzy	3	yzy	3	yzy	3	yzy
tie-in	1	x	<———		1	x	<———	
cross piece	2	ab	2	ba	2	ab	2	ba
spoke bottom	3	cba	3	abc	<———		———>	

The finish for this pin is the same as for the pin in Chapter 5 except without a fringe. It is repeated here briefly for your convenience.

The 14s7c flat net can be used as a pin with a tie-tack style fastener. This illustration shows top half of net only and is larger than actual size.

After the lace-up column, take off the stop bead and thread the tail needle onto the tail thread. Pass the tail needle down through the three beads of the 14th top spoke and tie off once. Using the working thread, go down through the first bead only of the first down column and tie off once. Make a loop in the blunt end of the 18 gauge wire with a pair of round-nosed pliers. Insert the 8 mm center bead into the interior of the flat net and squash the net flat, trapping the center bead in the holes formed by the top and bottom spokes. Insert the wire between two spokes, through the 8 mm bead and out between two spokes on the opposite side of the flat net. Make sure there are seven spokes on either side of the wire.

Hold the flat net in your left hand, making sure the center bead and ear wire stay in place, while you anchor the flat net using the working thread. After you have worked the anchoring thread all the way around the center bead, go down through the second and third bead of the first down-column and tie off. Finish by gluing the last knots on both the tail and working threads and cutting when dry or cutting to a quarter inch (6 mm) and burning down carefully.

Bend the 18 gauge wire to a 90° angle about 5 mm above the edge of the center bead. This will allow the tie-tack backing to lie flat on the flat net without overlapping the center bead which rather sticks out in the back.

9 More Baskets and Bottle Covers

This chapter contains five projects using very large spherical nets. The order in which they are presented may seem a little odd, but it was dictated by a need to put the bead chart for each project on a single page or on two facing pages. Two projects are baskets: one a rimless basket similar to the one you constructed in Chapter 6, and the other, a rimmed basket. Two projects are bottle covers: one for a 6 inch fat bottomed bottle with a long graceful neck and the other for a 4.5 inch bottleabout the size of an airline liquor bottle. The last project is for a Christmas tree ornament in the shape of a bell. The bottles and bell-shaped ornament can be purchased in home decorating and craft stores. See Appendix A for some sources.

—18s19c Rimless — Basket with Lining

This basket is very similar to, but a little larger than, the basket pattern detailed in Chapter 6. The patterns in this chapter have more interesting color patterns. The baskets are some of my favorite large spherical nets, I guess, because they stand up by themselves. The tension, however, is very, very important so you may want to review that section in Chapter 3. For the rimless basket you will need:

Thread: 3 or 4 lengths of size D Nymo or upholstery thread, each 72 inches long (cut as needed)

Needle: two thin but sturdy needles (John James #12 sharps)

Beads: Eight colors of size 11/0 seed beads. Avoid 2- and 3-cut beads. Choose one bead as a dark primary color and seven beads of a complementary secondary color that form a gradation of shades from dark to light. The primary color will be designated x. The seven secondary colors will be designated a, b, c, d, e, f and g. If you don't have seven colors, use as many as you have and repeat the last. For example, if you have five, use the lightest as e, f and g. For the lining use one of the seven secondary colors near the middle of the shade gradation and the primary color. These will be designated as d and x, respectively.

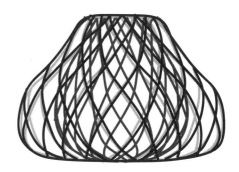

Rimless basket as seen from the side (about 3/4 scale). Individual beads are not shown but cross-piece sections are represented as solid lines that cross at the positions of the tie-in beads. A single layer of the exterior (darker lines) and of the lining (lighter lines) are shown.

Thread your needle and put on a stop bead, leaving a 6 inch tail. Use the chart below. Attach additional lengths of thread as needed as described in Chapter 6. This should be done in the lining section if possible. Finish the basket as described in Chapter 6.

Bead Chart for 18s19c Rimless Basket with Lining

	Section	1st Dn	1-17th Up	2-18th Dn	18th Up
Exterior	top	5 xxxxx	<———	5 xxxxx	<———-
	cross	2 xx	2 ba	2 xx	2 ba
	tie-in	1 x	1 x	<———	———>
	cross	3 abc	3 xxx	3 abc	3 xxx
	tie-in	1 x	<———	1 x	<———-
	cross	4 xxxx	4 dcba	4 xxxx	4 dcba
	tie-in	1 x	1 x	<———	———>
	cross	5 abcde	5 xxxxx	5 abcde	5 xxxxx
	tie-in	1 x	<———	1 x	<———-
	cross	6 xxxxxx	6 fedcba	6 xxxxxx	6 fedcba
	tie-in	1 x	1 x	<———	———>
	cross	7 abcdefg	7 xxxxxxx	7 abcdefg	7 xxxxxxx
	tie-in	1 x	<———	1 x	<———-
	cross	6 xxxxxx	6 fedcba	6 xxxxxx	6 fedcba
	tie-in	1 x	1 x	<———	———>
	cross	5 abcde	5 xxxxx	5 abcde	5 xxxxx
	tie-in	1 x	<———	1 x	<———-
	cross	4 xxxx	4 dcba	4 xxxx	4 dcba
	tie-in	1 x	1 x	<———	———>
	cross	3 abc	3 xxx	3 abc	3 xxx
	tie-in	1 x	<———	1 x	<———-
	cross	2 xx	2 ba	2 xx	2 ba
	tie-in	1 x	1 x	<———	———>
Lining	cross	2 dd	2 dd	2 dd	2 dd
	tie-in	1 x	<———	1 x	<———-
	cross	3 ddd	3 ddd	3 ddd	3 ddd
	tie-in	1 x	1 x	<———	———>
	cross	4 dddd	4 dddd	4 dddd	4 dddd
	tie-in	1 x	<———	1 x	<———-
	cross	5 ddddd	5 ddddd	5 ddddd	5 ddddd
	tie-in	1 x	1 x	<———	———>
	cross	5 ddddd	5 ddddd	5 ddddd	5 ddddd
	tie-in	1 x	<———	1 x	<———-
	cross	4 dddd	4 dddd	4 dddd	4 dddd
	tie-in	1 x	1 x	<———	———>
	cross	3 ddd	3 ddd	3 ddd	3 ddd
	tie-in	1 x	<———	1 x	<———-
	cross	2 dd	2 dd	2 dd	2 dd
	bottom	5 ddddd	5 ddddd	<———	———>

18s19c rimless basket in profile showing the exterior and lining portions of the spherical net (about 3/4 scale).

16s19c Bottle Cover

This bottle cover is for a cute 4.5 inch bottle I found at a Pier 1 store in Houston. See Appendix A. LOOK FOR THE LIST OF SUPPLIES YOU WILL NEED ON T HE NEXT PAGE. Sorry about the rearrangement.

Section	1st Dn	1-15th Up	2-16th Dn	16th Up
top	5 xxxxx	<———	5 xxxxx	<——--
cross	2 xx	2 ba	2 xx	2 ba
tie-in	1 x	1 x	<———	———>
cross	3 abc	3 xxx	3 abc	3 xxx
tie-in	1 x	<———	1 x	<——--
cross	4 xxxx	4 dcba	4 xxxx	4 dcba
tie-in	1 x	1 x	<———	———>
cross	5 abcde	5 xxxxx	5 abcde	5 xxxxx
tie-in	1 x	<———	1 x	<——--
cross	4 xxxx	4 dcba	4 xxxx	4 dcba
tie-in	1 x	1 x	<———	———>
cross	4 abcd	4 xxxx	4 abcd	4 xxxx
tie-in	1 x	<———	1 x	<——--
cross	4 xxxx	4 dcba	4 xxxx	4 dcba
tie-in	1 x	1 x	<———	———>
cross	3 abc	3 xxx	3 abc	3 xxx
tie-in	1 x	<———	1 x	<——--
cross	3 xxx	3 cba	3 xxx	3 cba
tie-in	1 x	1 x	<———	———>
cross	3 abc	3 xxx	3 abc	3 xxx
tie-in	1 x	<———	1 x	<——--
cross	3 xxx	3 cba	3 xxx	3 cba
tie-in	1 x	1 x	<———	———>
cross	3 abc	3 xxx	3 abc	3 xxx
tie-in	1 x	<———	1 x	<——--
cross	3 xxx	3 cba	3 xxx	3 cba
tie-in	1 x	1 x	<———	———>
cross	3 abc	3 xxx	3 abc	3 xxx
tie-in	1 x	<———	1 x	<——--
cross	4 xxxx	4 dcba	4 xxxx	4 dcba
tie-in	1 x	1 x	<———	———>
cross	4 abcd	4 xxxx	4 abcd	4 xxxx
tie-in	1 x	<———	1 x	<——--
cross	4 xxxx	4 dcba	4 xxxx	4 dcba
tie-in	1 x	1 x	<———	———>
cross	3 abc	3 xxx	3 abc	3 xxx
tie-in	1 x	<———	1 x	<——--
cross	2 xx	2 ba	2 xx	2 ba
bottom	3 xxx	3 xxx	<———	———>
extra	2 ab		2 ab	

Bead Chart for 16s19c Bottle Cover

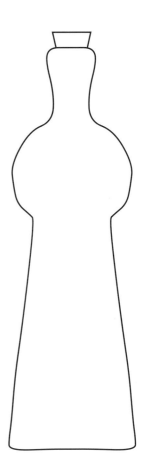

4.5 inch glass bottle with cork as seen from the side (about actual size).

For the bottle cover for the 4.5 inch bottle (bead chart above) you will need:

Thread: 2 lengths of size D Nymo or upholstery thread, each 72 inches long (cut as needed)

Needle: two thin but sturdy needles (John James #12 sharps)

Beads: Six colors of size 11/0 seed beads. Avoid 2- and 3-cut beads. Choose one bead as a dark primary color and five beads of complementary secondary colors that form a gradation of shades from dark to light. The primary color will be designated x. The five secondary colors will be designated a, b, c, d and e.

Thread your needle and put on a stop bead, leaving a 6 inch tail thread. Use the chart above. Attach additional lengths of thread as needed. This technique is described in Chapter 6. Remember that the top of the net will eventually go on the bottom of the bottle. Finish the bottle cover as described in Chapter 6 making sure to insert the bottle before finishing the lace-up column.

—18s23c Rimmed— Basket with Lining

This basket is similar the one above except the rim flares out. For the rimmed basket you will need:

Thread: 3 or 4 lengths of size D Nymo or upholstery thread, each 72 inches long (cut as needed)

Needle: two thin but sturdy needles (John James #12 sharps)

Beads: Seven colors of size 11/0 seed beads. Avoid 2- and 3-cut beads. Choose one bead as a dark primary color and six beads of complementary secondary colors that form a gradation of shades from dark to light. The primary color will be designated x. The six secondary colors will be designated a, b, c, d, e, and f. If you don't have six colors, use as many as you have and repeat the last. For example, if you have four, use the lightest as d, e, and f. For the lining use one of the six secondary colors near the middle of the shade gradation and the primary color. These will be designated as d and x, respectively.

Thread your needle and put on a stop bead, leaving a 6 inch tail thread. Use the chart on the next page. Attach additional lengths of thread as needed according to the description in Chapter 6. Attaching new threads should be done in the lining section if possible. Finish the basket as described in Chapter 6, by stuffing the lining down into the exterior of the basket and anchoring as usual.

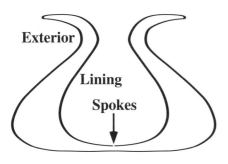

18s23c rimmed basket in profile showing the exterior and lining portions of the spherical net (about 3/4 scale).

Section	1st Dn	1-17th Up	2-18th Dn	18th Up
top	5 xxxxx	<———	5 xxxxx	<———
cross	2 xx	2 ba	2 xx	2 ba
tie-in	1 x	1 x	<———	———>
cross	3 abc	3 xxx	3 abc	3 xxx
tie-in	1 x	<———	1 x	<———
cross	4 xxxx	4 dcba	4 xxxx	4 dcba
tie-in	1 x	1 x	<———	———>
cross	5 abcde	5 xxxxx	5 abcde	5 xxxxx
tie-in	1 x	<———	1 x	<———
cross	6 xxxxxx	6 fedcba	6 xxxxxx	6 fedcba
tie-in	1 x	1 x	<———	———>
cross	6 abcdef	6 xxxxxx	6 abcdef	6 xxxxxx
tie-in	1 x	<———	1 x	<———
cross	5 xxxxx	5 edcba	5 xxxxx	5 edcba
tie-in	1 x	1 x	<———	———>
cross	4 abcd	4 xxxx	4 abcd	4 xxxx
tie-in	1 x	<———	1 x	<———
cross	3 xxx	3 cba	3 xxx	3 cba
tie-in	1 x	1 x	<———	———>
cross	2 ab	2 xx	2 ab	2 xx
tie-in	1 x	<———	1 x	<———
cross	3 xxx	3 cba	3 xxx	3 cba
tie-in	1 x	1 x	<———	———>
cross	4 abcd	4 xxxx	4 abcd	4 xxxx
tie-in	1 x	<———	1 x	<———
cross	5 xxxxx	5 edcba	5 xxxxx	5 edcba
tie-in	1 x	1 x	<———	———>
cross	4 dddd	4 dddd	4 dddd	4 dddd
tie-in	1 x	<———	1 x	<———
cross	3 ddd	3 ddd	3 ddd	3 ddd
tie-in	1 x	1 x	<———	———>
cross	2 dd	2 dd	2 dd	2 dd
tie-in	1 x	<———	1 x	<———
cross	3 ddd	3 ddd	3 ddd	3 ddd
tie-in	1 x	1 x	<———	———>
cross	4 dddd	4 dddd	4 dddd	4 dddd
tie-in	1 x	<———	1 x	<———
cross	5 ddddd	5 ddddd	5 ddddd	5 ddddd
tie-in	1 x	1 x	<———	———>
cross	5 ddddd	5 ddddd	5 ddddd	5 ddddd
tie-in	1 x	<———	1 x	<———
cross	4 dddd	4 dddd	4 dddd	4 dddd
tie-in	1 x	1 x	<———	———>
cross	3 ddd	3 ddd	3 ddd	3 ddd
tie-in	1 x	<———	1 x	<———
cross	2 dd	2 dd	2 dd	2 dd
bottom	5 ddddd	5 ddddd	<———	———>

Exterior

Lining

Bead Chart for 18s23c Rimmed Basket with Lining

14s33c Bottle Cover

This bottle cover is for a very gracefully shaped bottle that I have seen in a few home decoration stores for $3-$4 (see Appendix A). The first one I made is on the front cover. The bottle is dark blue and has a matte finish. I have seen a few other colors both with and without matte finishes. For this bottle cover you will need:

Thread: 3 or 4 lengths of size D Nymo or upholstery thread, each 72 inches long (cut as needed)

Needle: two thin but sturdy needles (John James #12 sharps)

Beads: Eight colors of size 11/0 seed beads. Avoid 2- and 3-cut beads. Choose one bead as a dark primary color and seven beads of complementary secondary colors that form a gradation of shades from dark to light. The primary color will be designated x. The seven secondary colors will be designated a, b, c, d, e, f and g.

Bead Chart for 14s33c Bottle Cover

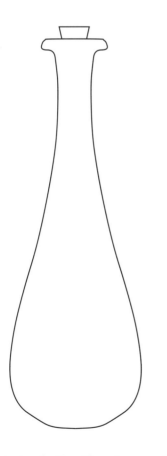

Six inch glass bottle with cork as seen from the side (about 3/4 scale).

Section	1st Dn	1-13th Up	2-14th Dn	14th Up
top	5 xxxxx	<————	5 xxxxx	<————-
cross	2 xx	2 ba	2 xx	2 ba
tie-in	1 x	1 x	<————	————>
cross	3 abc	3 xxx	3 abc	3 xxx
tie-in	1 x	<————	1 x	<————-
cross	4 xxxx	4 dcba	4 xxxx	4 dcba
tie-in	1 x	1 x	<————	————>
cross	5 abcde	5 xxxxx	5 abcde	5 xxxxx
tie-in	1 x	<————	1 x	<————-
cross	6 xxxxxx	6 fedcba	6 xxxxxx	6 fedcba
tie-in	1 x	1 x	<————	————>
cross	7 abcdefg	7 xxxxxxx	7 abcdefg	7 xxxxxxx
tie-in	1 x	<————	1 x	<————-
cross	6 xxxxxx	6 fedcba	6 xxxxxx	6 fedcba
tie-in	1 x	1 x	<————	————>
cross	6 abcdef	6 xxxxxx	6 abcdef	6 xxxxxx
tie-in	1 x	<————	1 x	<————-
cross	5 xxxxx	5 edcba	5 xxxxx	5 edcba
tie-in	1 x	1 x	<————	————>
cross	5 abcde	5 xxxxx	5 abcde	5 xxxxx
tie-in	1 x	<————	1 x	<————-
cross	4 xxxx	4 dcba	4 xxxx	4 dcba
tie-in	1 x	1 x	<————	————>
cross	4 abcd	4 xxxx	4 abcd	4 xxxx
tie-in	1 x	<————	1 x	<————-
cross	4 xxxx	4 dcba	4 xxxx	4 dcba
tie-in	1 x	1 x	<————	————>
cross	3 abc	3 xxx	3 abc	3 xxx

tie-in	1 x	<————	1 x	<———--
cross	3 xxx	3 cba	3 xxx	3 cba
tie-in	1 x	1 x	<————	————>
cross	3 abc	3 xxx	3 abc	3 xxx
tie-in	1 x	<————	1 x	<———--
cross	3 xxx	3 cba	3 xxx	3 cba
tie-in	1 x	1 x	<————	————>
cross	3 ab	2 xx	2 ab	2 xx
tie-in	1 x	<————	1 x	<———--
cross	2 xx	2 ba	2 xx	2 ba
tie-in	1 x	1 x	<————	————>
cross	2 ab	2 xx	2 ab	2 xx
tie-in	1 x	<————	1 x	<———--
cross	2 xx	2 ba	2 xx	2 ba
tie-in	1 x	1 x	<————	————>
cross	2 ab	2 xx	2 ab	2 xx
tie-in	1 x	<————	1 x	<———--
cross	2 xx	2 ba	2 xx	2 ba
tie-in	1 x	1 x	<————	————>
cross	2 ab	1 xx	1 ab	1 xx
tie-in	1 x	<————	1 x	<———--
cross	1 x	1 a	1 x	1 a
tie-in	1 x	1 x	<————	————>
cross	1 a	1 x	1 a	1 x
tie-in	1 x	<————	1 x	<———--
cross	1 x	1 a	1 x	1 a
tie-in	1 x	1 x	<————	————>
cross	1 a	1 x	1 a	1 x
tie-in	1 x	<————	1 x	<———--
cross	1 x	1 a	1 x	1 a
tie-in	1 x	1 x	<————	————>
cross	1 a	1 x	1 a	1 x
tie-in	1 x	<————	1 x	<———--
cross	1 x	1 a	1 x	1 a
tie-in	1 x	1 x	<————	————>
cross	1 a	1 x	1 a	1 x
tie-in	1 x	<————	1 x	<———--
cross	1 x	1 a	1 x	1 a
bottom	5 xxxxx	5 xxxxx	<————	————>
extra	2 ab		2 ab	

Thread your needle and put on a stop bead, leaving a 6 inch tail thread. Use the chart above. Attach additional lengths of thread as needed. This technique is described in Chapter 6. Remember that the top of the net will eventually go on the bottom of the bottle. Finish the bottle cover as described in Chapter 6 making sure to insert the bottle before finishing the lace-up column.

17s13c Christmas— Tree Ornament Cover

This ornament cover is for a bell-shaped clear glass Christmas tree ornament I found at a local craft store just before last Christmas. See Appendix A. For this ornament cover you will need:

Thread: 2 lengths of size D Nymo or upholstery thread, each 72 inches long (cut as needed)

Needle: two thin but sturdy needles (John James #12 sharps)

Beads: Four colors of size 11/0 seed beads: red, green or emerald, crystal and gold. Avoid 2- and 3-cut beads.

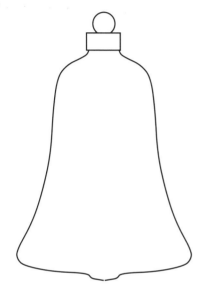

Glass Christmas bell ornament as seen from the side (about 3/4 scale).

Section	1st Dn	1-16th Up	2-17th Dn	17th Up
top	5 green	<————	5 green	<————-
cross	2 red	2 red	2 red	2 red
tie-in	1 green	1 gold	<————	————>
cross	3 cryst	3 cryst	3 cryst	3 cryst
tie-in	1 gold	<————	1 gold	<————-
cross	4 red	4 red	4 red	4 red
tie-in	1 gold	1 gold	<————	————>
cross	5 green	4 green	4 green	4 green
tie-in	1 gold	<————	1 gold	<————-
cross	4 red	4 red	4 red	4 red
tie-in	1 gold	1 gold	<————	————>
cross	3 cryst	3 cryst	3 cryst	3 cryst
tie-in	1 gold	<————	1 gold	<————-
cross	3 green	3 green	3 green	3 green
tie-in	1 gold	1 gold	<————	————>
cross	3 red	3 red	3 red	3 red
tie-in	1 gold	<————	1 gold	<————-
cross	3 green	3 green	3 green	3 green
tie-in	1 gold	1 gold	<————	————>
cross	3 red	3 red	3 red	3 red
tie-in	1 gold	<————	1 gold	<————-
cross	3 green	3 green	3 green	3 green
tie-in	1 gold	1 gold	<————	————>
cross	3 cryst	3 cryst	3 cryst	3 cryst
tie-in	1 gold	<————	1 gold	<————-
cross	2 red	2 red	2 red	2 red
bottom	5 green	5 green	<————	————>
extra	1 gold		1 gold	

Thread your needle and put on a stop bead, leaving a 6 inch tail thread. Use the chart above. Attach additional lengths of thread as needed. This technique is described in Chapter 6. Remember that the top of the net will eventually go on the bottom of the ornament. Finish the ornament cover as described in Chapter 6 making sure to insert the ornament before finishing the lace-up column.

Afterword

Now you know almost everything I know about spherical nets. I would love to hear from you, to know how you like the techniques and patterns and how you liked the book. Mostly, I would like to know any ideas you have for improving or extending the use of spherical nets.

Now that the book is finished, I will let my computer and family have a little break before plunging into my next writing projects. This time they will be individual spherical net patterns on 4 to 6 pages that are punched to fit into a loose leaf notebook. Project ideas include patterns for hair barrettes, more Christmas tree ornaments, more bottle covers, baskets with covers and necklaces made with covered beads and bagels (similar to a flat net but shaped like a donut or bagel). If you have an idea or request for a pattern or have made a spherical net pattern you would like to share with other, please let me know and we can work something out.

I can be reached at my store, Bazillion Beautiful Beads, 3904 Old College Road, Bryan, Texas 77801, (409) 846-9120. And if you are ever in this area, please stop by and talk to me about beads.

Appendix A: Sources for Supplies

Most of the beads, tools and supplies mentioned in this book are available from a variety of places. My own bead shop, Bazillion Beautiful Beads, (BBB), carries most of these things or can order them. BBB will handle small quantities and there is no minimum order. For larger quantities of some beads and supplies, two bead stores are recommended: Shipwreck Beads in Olympia, Washington, and General Beads in San Francisco and San Diego. General Beads has a wonderful selection of Japanese seed beads. Shipwreck Beads has a comprehensive selection of Czechoslovakian seed and larger (4 to 12 mm glass) beads. Both Shipwreck and General Beads have catalogs for small fees. Indian Jewelers Supply (IJS), in Gallup and Albuquerque, NM, has a wonderful supply of tools, precious and base metals in wires and sheets and stone and shell beads.

Category	Description	Sources
Bead Gauge		BBB, larger bead shops
Beads	seed	larger bead shops, General Beads (Japanese), Shipwreck Beads (Czech)
	4-6 mm	most bead shops, Shipwreck Beads
	5 mm	BBB, Shipwreck Beads
	Swarovsky Crystal	BBB, General Beads
	huge - 16 to 20 mm	BBB, wooden and plastic in some bead & craft shops
	2-3 mm gold & silver colored	BBB, General Beads
Bottles	6 inch tapered	BBB, Pier 1, Bed, Bath & Beyond
	4.5 inch shaped	BBB, Pier 1
	White Out® or Liquid Paper®	office supply stores, friends who work in offices
Crimp beads	for stick pins	BBB, most bead shops
Crimper tool	for crimping crimps	BBB, General Beads
Ear studs	4 mm cup	BBB
	6 mm flat	BBB, many bead & craft shops, General Beads
Ear backs	comfort clutch	BBB, many bead & craft shops
Ear clips	for hanging	BBB, many bead & craft shops, General Beads
	15 mm sew on pad	BBB, some bead & craft shops
Glue	watch crystal glue	BBB, jewelers supply stores
	clear nail polish	anywhere
Head Pins	3 inch stiff for stick pins	BBB and supplies are limited. These were discontinued because everybody complained they were too stiff. I bought up remaining stock.
Jump rings	4 mm outer diameter	BBB
Needles	1.125 inch John James #12	BBB, Shipwreck Beads
	2 inch #13	BBB, most bead shops that carry seed beads, Shipwreck Beads

Ornament	bell-shaped, Christmas tree	BBB, some craft stores before Christmas
Pin backs	sew-on	BBB, many craft stores
Pliers	round nose or rosary	BBB, jewelers supplies, General Beads
	Chain or needle nose	BBB, jewelers supplies, General Beads
	wire cutters	BBB, jewelers supplies, General Beads
Sandpaper	200 to 400 grit black carbide	most hardware stores
Solder	Staybright® by J.W. Harris Co.	BBB, some jewelry supply stores
Soldering iron	small tip with wire stand	most hardware stores
Starter kits		BBB, contains five John James #12 sharps, two bobbicontains 5 #12 short sharp needles, 2 bobbins of size D Nymo thread (black and white), twelve 4 mm soldered rings, six 4 mm cup studs, six 6 mm flat studs, six 28 mm lengths of 20 gauge, gold-filled, half hard wire, 18 comfort clutches, 4 sharpened 2.75 stiff head pins with ear clutches, two 1 inch sharpened lengths of 18 gauge brass wire with 2 tie tack backs.
Thread	Upholstery	most material shops
	Nymo	BBB, many bead & craft shops, General Beads, Shipwreck Beads.
Tie tack backs	for stud pins	BBB, some craft & rock shops
Tweezers		BBB, many bead shops, General Beads
Wire	Gold filled, half hard, 20 gauge	BBB for short lengths, IJS for long lengths
	Silver, half hard, 20 gauge	BBB for short lengths, IJS for long lengths
	Brass or nickle, 18 gauge	BBB for short lengths, IJS for long lengths
	Brass or nickle, 20 gauge	BBB for short lengths, also available in some bead and craft shops on spools.

Bazillion Beautiful Beads
3904 Old College Road
Bryan, Texas 77802
(409) 846-9120
See price list
No minimum order

Shipwreck Beads
2727 Westmoor CT. SW
Olympia, WA 98502
Information (206) 754-2323
Orders only (800) 950-4232
http://www.shipwreck.com/
Catalog $3.00
Minimum order $25.00

General Beads
317 National City Blvd.
National City, CA 91950
Voice (619) 336-0100
FAX (800) 572-1302
Catalog $4.00
Minimum order $20.00

Bed, Bath and Beyond
(In most major U.S. cities)
Corporate Headquarters
715 Morris Turnpike
Springfield, NJ 07081
(516) 420-7050 ask for receptionist or dial "0" for operator

Pier 1 Imports
(Many stores throughout the U.S. Check local phone book for one nearest you)
http://www.pier1.com/

Indian Jewelry Supplies
601 East Coal
Gallup, NM 87301-6005
in NM (505) 722-4451
FAX (505) 722-4172
Orders (800) 545-6540
Catalogs $6.00 set or $3.00 each (Tools & Supplies, Findings & Metals, Stones)

Bazillion Beautiful Beads

Phone (409) 846-9120

Bryan, TX 77802

Bazillion Beautiful Beads (BBB) is a retail bead store that will sell small quantities of any bead, tool or supply mentioned in this book. The mail-order service is for the convenience of book owners who may want to try out some of the patterns before making a large investment in supplies. Some items, such as the jump rings for central stud earrings, are difficult to find in the precisely correct size. BBB guarantees the size of their 4 mm jump rings. The head pins used for stick pins in this book and sold by BBB are much stiffer than those usually found in bead and craft stores. If something you need is not in this list, describe it in your order and BBB will try to find it for you. Call with your order or use the order form on the back page of this book.

Bead Gauge —for measuring the outer diameter of beads in millimeters and inches.

T1001	12.00

Beads —5 mm round glass beads. In red, sapphire, dark topaz, emerald, capri blue, clear, opal pink, black, purple, and aqua. Specify color. Strand of 50 beads, one color.

B2001	1.75

Beads —5 mm faceted glass beads. In red, sapphire, dark topaz, emerald, capri blue, clear, opal pink, black, purple, and aqua. Specify color. Strand of 50 beads, one color.

B2002	2.00

Beads —5 mm round faceted Swarovski crystal beads. In red, sapphire, emerald, capri blue, clear, purple, light pink, fushia and aqua. Specify color. Bag of 20 beads, one color.

B2003	4.00

Beads —huge (16 - 20 mm) in various colors and materials. Call for availability and pricing.

Beads —gold colored, 2.5 mm, bag of 100.

B2011	3.00

Beads —gold colored, 3.0 mm, bag of 100.

B2012	4.00

Beads —silver colored, 2.5 mm, bag of 100.

B2021	3.00

Beads —silver colored, 3.0 mm, bag of 100.

B2022	4.00

Bottles —6 inches tall, gracefully tapered, matte finish, in dark blue and purple. See picture next page. Specify color.

S3001	6.00

Bottles —6 inches tall, gracefully tapered, regular shiny finish, in cobalt blue and coke bottle green. See picture next page. Specify color.

S3002	5.00

Bottles —4.5 inches tall, somewhat shaped, regular shiny finish, in coke bottle green. See picture next page.

S3003	2.00

Crimp Beads —for holding beads on stick pins. Gold color.

Bag of 20 beads.

S3011	1.00

Half ounce bag.

S3012	7.00

Crimping Tool —for crimping crimp beads.

T1002	14.00

Ear studs —4 mm cup studs in surgical steel.

Bag of 10

S3021	1.00

Bag of 100

S3022	5.00

Ear studs —6 mm flat base studs in surgical steel.

Bag of 10

S3031	1.00

Bag of 100

S3032	4.00

Comfort clutch earring backs —gold colored and surgical steel with plastic collar. Bag of 100

S3035	3.00

Ear clips—spring back with ball and loop for hanging. Gold color. Bag of 10.

S3051	3.00

Ear clips—15 mm perforated base for sewing. Gold colored. Bag of 10.

S3052	2.00

Glue—fine watch crystal glue.

S3060	6.00

Head pins —2.75 inches, very stiff, gold colored, NOT sharpened.

Bag of 10.

S3071	1.00

Half oz bag.

S3072	3.00

Jump rings —4 mm outer diameter for central stud earrings, gold colored. NOT soldered.

Package of 25.
S3081   1.00
Half ounce bag.
S3082   3.00

Needles —1.125 inches, John James #12 sharps. Package of 25.

S3110   4.00

Needles —2 inches, #13. Package of 25.

S3115   5.00

Ornaments—Glass, bell-shaped, 2.5 inches tall, 2 inches diameter at base. See picture this page. Each.

S3004   2.00

Pin backs—rhodium plate, one inch, sew-on back. Bag of 10.

S3040   1.50

Pliers —round nosed or rosary pliers. 4.5 inches long.

T1003   12.50

Pliers —chain nosed (also called needle nose). 4.5 inches long.

T1004   12.50

Pliers —wire cutters. 4.5 inches long.

T1005   12.50

Solder kit —Stay-brite, package contains 1/2 troy ounce of solder and 1/2 fluid ounce of flux and instructions. Does NOT include soldering iron.

S3120   6.00

Spherical net starter kit—contains 5 #12 short sharp needles, 2 bobbins of size D Nymo thread (black and white), twelve 4 mm soldered rings, six 4 mm cup studs, six 6 mm flat studs, six 28 mm lengths of 20 gauge, gold-filled, half hard wire, 18 comfort clutches, 4 sharpened 2.75 stiff head pins with ear clutches, two 1 inch sharpened lengths of 18 gauge brass wire with 2 tie tack backs.

S3200   10.00

Thread—size D Nymo on bobbins. Black or white. Specify color.

S3120   1.00

Tie tack backs—also called tie tack keepers or butterfly backs. Bag of 10

S3091   1.50

Tweezers—4.5 inches. sharp point.

T1006   7.00

Wire—gold filled, half hard, 20 gauge. 12 inch length.

S3130   3.00

Wire—silver, half hard, 20 gauge. 12 inch length.

S3135   3.00

Wire—20 gauge, brass (golden) or nickel. Specify color.

12 inch length
S3141   0.25
20 foot roll
S3142   2.00

Wire—18 gauge, brass (golden) or nickel. Specify color.

12 inch length
S3146   0.25
20 foot roll
S3147   2.00

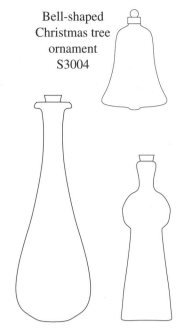

Bell-shaped Christmas tree ornament S3004

6 inch tapered bottle, S3001 &S3002

4.5 inch, somewhat shaped bottle S3003

Appendix B: Bead Graphs

This appendix contains spherical net bead graphs for all of the projects in the book. They are labeled by their formal names with reference to use and chapter. Bead graphs for some of the larger projects were reduced to fit on a single page. You might increase the size of the graphs when you copy them.

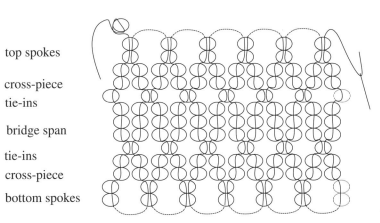

top spokes

cross-piece
tie-ins

bridge span

tie-ins
cross-piece

bottom spokes

Side-ways bead graph for a ball net to cover a 12 mm bead. The thread shows the direction of construction from upper left to upper right. Dotted beads in rightmost column are repeats of spokes and tie-ins on first column.

The graphs are of two types: the first is a side-ways, flat view which was introduced in Chapter 2, and the second is a "finished" view. The side-ways view shows the sequence of beads as they are added to the spherical net. The figure to the right shows that you always start in the upper left-hand corner where the tail thread and stop-bead are located. This figure shows the thread going through the sequence of 6 down- and 6 up-columns. The dotted threads between the spokes are shown loose, but are really very tight. This was necessary to make the figure flat. In the pages that follow the bead graphs do not have the thread showing, but for all of them you start at the upper left and finish at the upper right.

Finished view of a ball net to cover a 12 mm bead.

The "finished" views are shown with the side-ways views to give you an idea of what the finished product will look like. Unfortunately, these three-dimensional figures are difficult to represent in two dimensions. For the ball nets, one side of the solid figure is shown. For the flat nets, both a two-sided figure and a one-sided figure are shown. The latter represents the top half of the net and the bridge span.

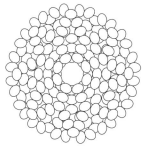

Finished view of a flat net showing both the top and bottom.

The purpose of these graphs is twofold: to give you a visual analog of the bead charts in Chapters 7 through 9 and to provide graphs you can color to try out new color schemes. For this reason the pages in Appendix B ONLY may be photocopied FOR USE ONLY BY THE OWNER OF THIS BOOK. No other part of this book may be photocopied or reproduced in any manner. Photocopies of the bead graphs in Appendix B may not be sold or distributed in any manner. Any reproduction of the contents of this book, except that expressly stated above, is a violation of copyright laws.

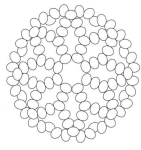

Finished view of a flat net showing only the top half of the net and the bridge spans.

6s3c ball net to cover a 12 mm bead (Chapters 2 & 7)

6s3c ball net to cover a 16 mm bead (Chapter 7)

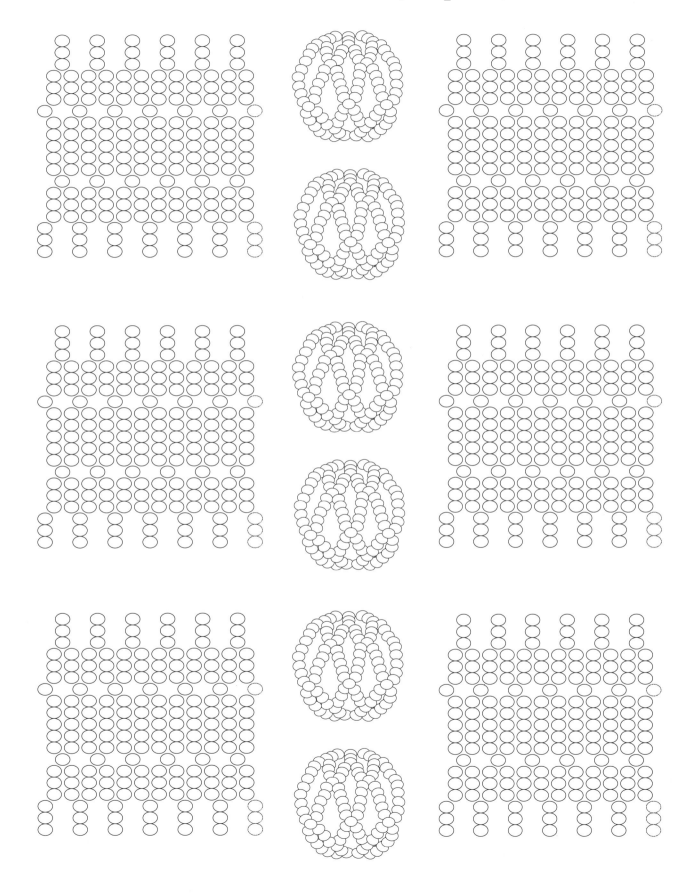

8s3c ball net to cover a 16 mm bead (Chapter 7)

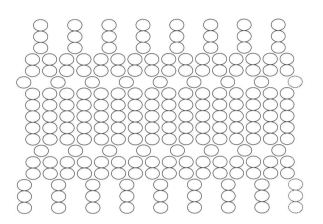

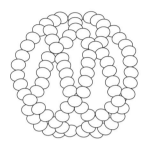

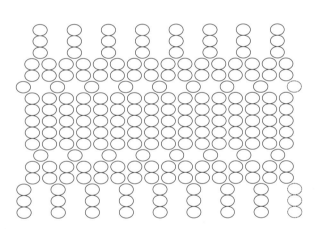

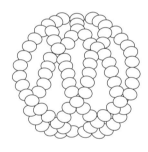

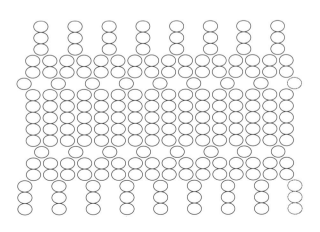

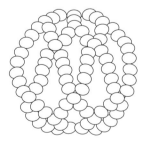

10s5c ball net to cover a 20 mm bead (Chapter 7)

6s5c drop net for earrings (Chapter 7)

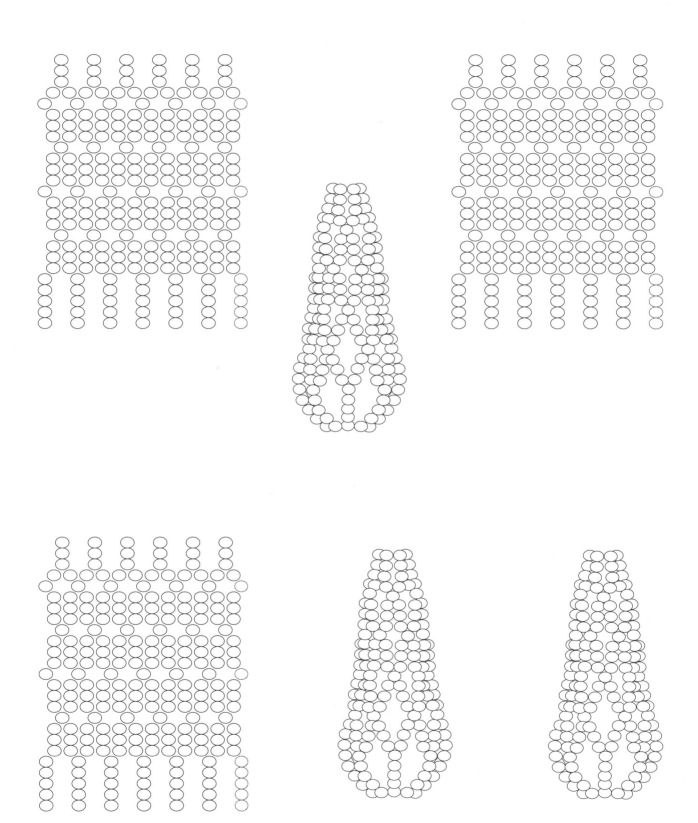

10s1c flat net (collar) for top of drop net earrings (Chapter 7)

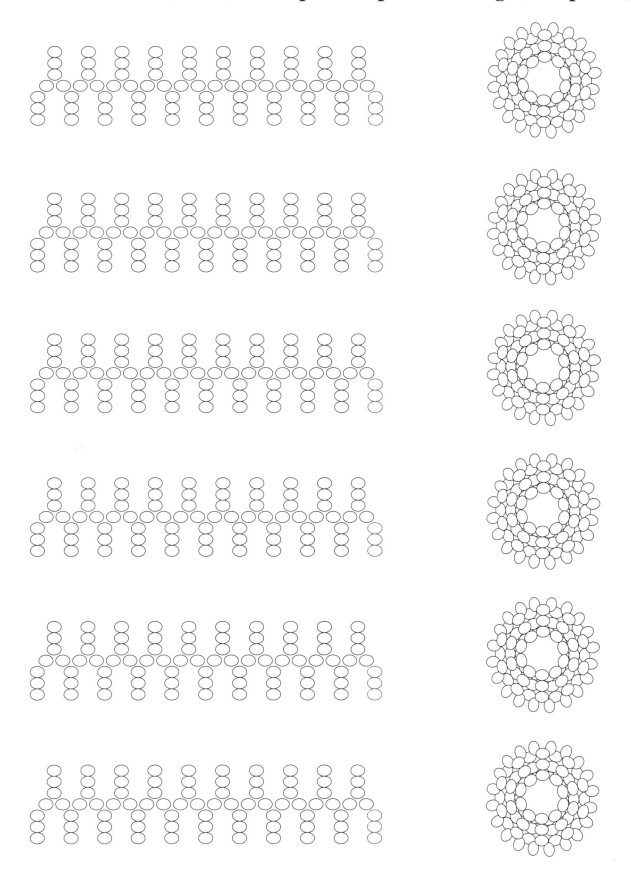

8s3c flat net for anchoring and jump rings (Chapters 3 & 4)

8s3c flat net for top of fringed earrings (Chapter 8)

8s5c flat net for central stud earrings (Chapter 8)

10s5c flat net for off-center stud earrings (Chapter 8)

12s5c flat net for off-center stud earrings (Chapters 5 & 8)

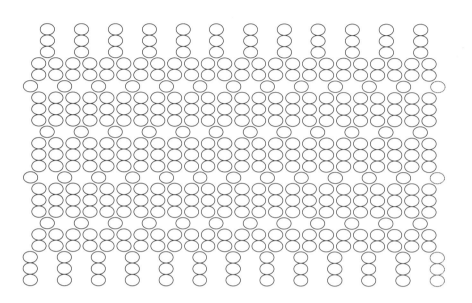

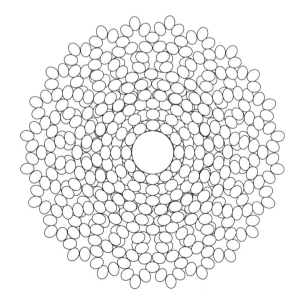

14s5c flat net for off-center stud earrings (Chapter 8)

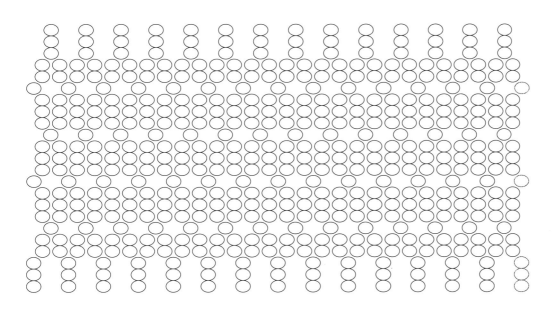

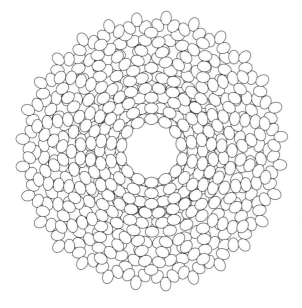

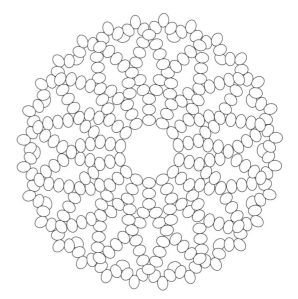

10s7c flat net for off-center stud earrings & pin (Chapter 8)

14s7c flat net for tie-tack pin (Chapters 5 & 8)

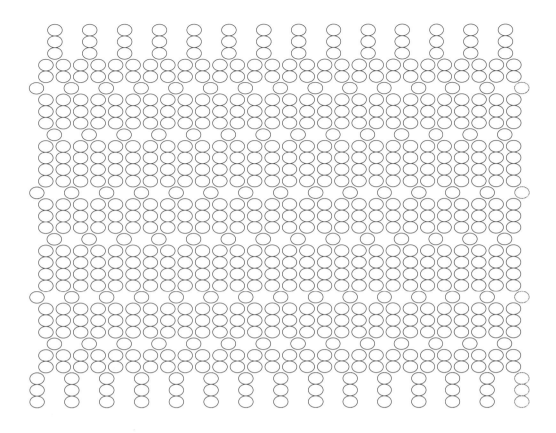

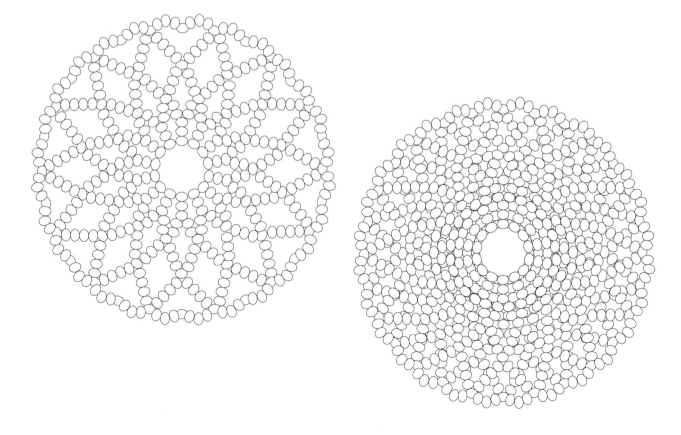

18s15c rimless basket (Chapter 6)

18s19c rimless basket (Chapter 9)

18s23c rimmed basket (Chapter 9)

16s11c Liquid Paper bottle cover (Chapter 6)

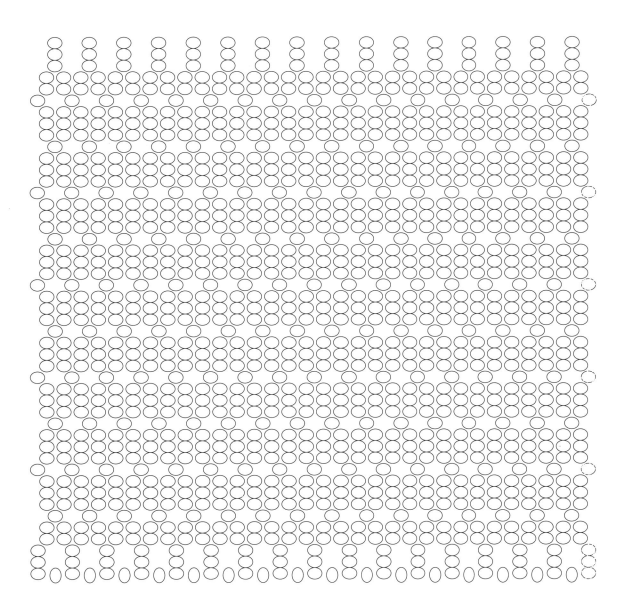

16s19c 4.5 inch bottle cover (Chapter 9)

14s33c 6 inch tapered bottle cover (Chapter 9)

17s13c bell-shaped Christmas tree ornament cover (Chapter 9)

Glossary

Anchoring	The process by which the two sets of spokes are sewn together. Used in baskets and flat nets.
Ball net	Spherical net with an interior bead.
Basket	Spherical net (usually rather large) that is shaped like a basket with an external layer of beads and an internal layer of beads called the lining.
Bead Gauge	A handy tool for measuring the outer diameter of beads, jump rings and other small objects. Scales in millimeters and fractions of inches.
Bottle covers	Spherical net (usually rather large) that covers a bottle, ornament or other object.
Bridge-span	Part of a spherical net made up of beads through which the thread passes only once. Usually at the edge of a flat net or in the middle of a ball net. Not all spherical nets have bridge-spans. See Parts, spherical net.
Column	Part of a spherical net made up of all the beads between and included in the two sets of spokes. A column is either a down-column or an up-column, depending on which direction your needle is pointing as it is constructed. Spoke and tie-in beads are shared between an up- and down-column, while a cross-piece or bridge-span belongs to only one column.
Crimp bead	A small gold or silver colored metal bead with cerrations on the outer surface. Made to be flattened with a crimping tool or pliers to hold beading wire in place. Used in this book to hold beads on wires or head pins used as pinning devices for large flat nets.
Crimping tool	A special type of pliers for mashing crimp beads. With regular pliers, the mashed crimp bead is flat and may stick out and scratch. A crimping tool has two sets of grooves where the crimp bead is first flattened into a U-shaped band and then folded over into a round ball.
Cross-piece	Part of a spherical net made up of beads through which the thread passes only once. See Parts, spherical net.

Dangle	One of several columns of beads that hangs from a small flat net to make an earring or from a large flat net to make a pin. The group of dangles on one flat net is also refered to as a fringe.
Drop net	A tear-drop shaped spherical net that covers a tear-drop shaped interior bead or a column of beads on a head pin.
Flat net	Flattened spherical net. A two sided beaded disk used to make earrings and pins. Fringes can be attached.
Head pin	A 2 or 3 inch length of wire with a small metal disk soldered on one end. Stiff head pins are used as pining devices for large flat net pins.
Jump ring	A small loop of wire, usually round. In central stud flat net earrings soldered jump rings (4 mm O.D.) hold the ear stud in place.
Parts, spherical net	Spherical nets are made up of spokes, cross-pieces, bridge-spans and tie-in beads. The number and size of each type of part depends on the final application of the spherical net.

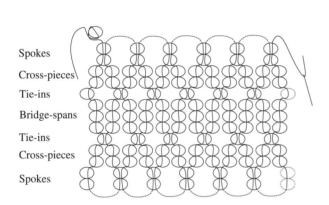

Spokes
Cross-pieces
Tie-ins
Bridge-spans
Tie-ins
Cross-pieces
Spokes

Spherical net parts as seen from the side.

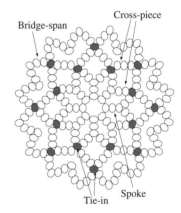

Bridge-span
Cross-piece
Tie-in
Spoke

Spherical net parts as seen from the top of a flat net.

Spherical net	A net made of seed beads and thread which starts out in a more or less spherical shape. Final shape depends on application. Spherical nets can be flattended to form two sided disks or put around beads or other objects as covers.
Spokes	Part of a spherical net made up of beads through which the thread passes twice. All spherical nets have two sets of spokes, one at the top and the other at the bottom of the net. See Parts, spherical net.
Stop bead	Temporary bead with a simple knot around it to hold the first column of beads on a spherical net in place. Separates the "tail thread" from the "working thread". Taken off after the body of the spherical net is finished and before a second needle is threaded onto the the tail thread to finish tying off.

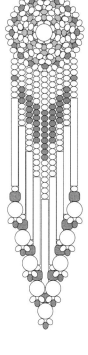

Tail needle

A second needle that is threaded onto the tail thread after the body of the spherical net is finished in order to tie off the tail thread.

Tail thread

The part of the thread on the other side of the stop bead from the needle.

Tension

Force excerted on the beads of a spherical net by the thread. For all spherical nets, especially large ones, tension should be kept as tight as possible.

Tie-in

Part of a spherical net made up of beads through which the thread passes twice. See Parts, spherical net. Not to be confused with "tie off". Tie-ins do not involve making knots.

Tie off

The process of tying knots and hiding the ends of the thread (both tail and working threads) in the body of a flat net after it is finished. A knot can be glued and the thread cut short when the glue is dry or the thread can be cut to 1/4 inch and burned down carefully with a paper match. Be sure to dispose of the match in a container other than a waste-paper basket.

Working thread

The part of the thread on the same side of the stop bead as the primary needle. The primary needle is also called the working needle.

Some types of spherical nets

Ball net

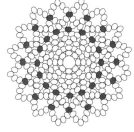

Flat net

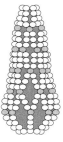

Drop net

Flat net with dangles

Index

**azillion
eautiful
B EADS**

3904 Old College Road
Bryan, Texas 77801

(409) 846-9120

Ordered by:

Name _____

Address _____

City _____ State _____ Zip _____

Daytime telephone number __(_____)_____

Method of payment: Check/Money Order_____ COD_____

VISA/MC/AE ☐☐☐☐☐☐☐☐☐☐☐☐☐☐☐☐

Exp. Date ☐☐ – ☐☐

Signature as on card_____

Item No.	Quantity	Part Number	Description	Color if applicable	Unit Price	Total

Shipping and Handling Charges			
$0 to $29.99	$4.95	Subtotal	
$30 to $59.99	$5.95	Texas residents add 8.25% sales tax	
$60 to $89.99	$6.95	Shipping and Handling	
OVER $90.00	$7.95	COD charge (if applicable) 4.95	
COD charge	$4.95	Total of Order	